To Cori,

Ultimate Tragedy

DOREEN PCHAJEK

Doreen Pchajek
May 1, 2015

ISBN -10:1508586160
ISBN-13: 978-1508586166

DEDICATION

This book is dedicated to the loving memory of my daughter, Stacey, who had always praised my writing skills and encouraged me to write a book.

ACKNOWLEDGMENTS

I would like to express my sincere gratitude to Marianne Curtis for everything she did to help make this second edition possible. I absolutely love how she redesigned the cover so that Stacey is the first thing you see when you look at the book. Marianne has done a lot to help promote my book, including putting it on Amazon. I appreciate the fact that she saw the need for this story to get out there and took the initiative to make that happen.

AUTHORS NOTE

I've been procrastinating about writing this book for five long years. So much has happened in these past five years that it's hard to know where to begin. Although I am surrounded by people who love me dearly, I now feel very much alone most of the time. That is one of the biggest reasons why I decided to write this book. I want others who have experienced the 'Ultimate Tragedy' to know that they are not alone. It's true that nobody else can possibly know what another person is feeling, but those of us who've experienced the 'Ultimate Tragedy' share an unspoken connection. We feel that we can relate better to someone who has experienced something similar to us.

I have titled this book the "Ultimate Tragedy" because I believe that there is no greater tragedy that one could experience but the loss of a child. Nothing could ever compare to the complicity of emotions and the pain involved with losing a child. If you have experienced the loss of a child, you will know what I'm talking about and hopefully this book will help you to realize that you are not alone and maybe some of my experiences will help you try to move on. Even if you have not experienced this yourself, reading this book will help you to understand what other people who have experienced it go through as they try to move on with this devastating void in their lives.

It has taken me a long time to get to where I am today. I will never **"*get over it*"** and I will never bring **"*closure*"** to it. In my training as a nurse, I had learned about the grieving process so I should've been prepared...**wrong!** Nothing could ever prepare someone for this. Please don't ever tell someone going through this that they need to **"*get over it*"** or that they need to bring **"*closure*"** to it. We will never get over it and as for the word "closure".I hate that word! We don't want that part of our life to end or be finished. That child was and always will be a part of our lives and we cannot close the door and get over it. Some people who were very well meaning would tell me that I needed to get over it and move on with my life. Professionals tended to use the word "closure". To me, hearing someone say that I needed to bring closure to it, was no different than someone saying "get over it". All good intentions aside, this is not helpful.

This book is based on what I have gone through in the past six years and none of it is made up. It should leave you with a greater understanding on the subject and hopefully that knowledge will enable you or someone you know to live a life that's not in darkness.

DOREEN PCHAJEK

CHAPTER ONE

THE DAY THAT CHANGED MY LIFE

My life, as I knew it, changed forever on the morning of May 27, 1998. The day started out much like any other day. We were totally unaware of the tragedy that awaited us. In fact, if somebody would've told me what was going to happen I'm certain that I would've thought they were nuts. Those kinds of things happen to other people, not to us. In retrospect, now I can see that there were signs. Little warning signs that for whatever reason I didn't see at the time.

My husband Bob and I were getting ready for work. Bob had been a flooring installer for the past 20 years. It was in January of 1998 that he and a partner with whom he had worked for a number of years decided to open their own floor store. His partner, Debbie looked after the sales while Bob took care of the installations. I had recently done the RN Refresher course and returned to work in February of 1998 after being off work since February of 1991 when I was involved in a motor vehicle accident. Although my injuries were not that serious, I was not healing like I should have been and was subsequently diagnosed with Chronic Fatigue Syndrome/ Fibromyalgia. It was a long, hard struggle but I was determined to be able to return to nursing. I think that I also thought it was an important lesson to teach my kids about not giving up and setting goals. I had always done nursing in a hospital before, but now I was doing Homecare and I was thoroughly enjoying it.

Cory, our eldest son (age 18) was sleeping in that morning. He had just come back home at the end of April after spending his first year in residence at university. The university is only a forty-five minute drive from our home, but we thought it would be easier for him if he didn't have to travel back and forth. As it turned out, that was a big mistake on our part. Cory had a very chaotic and confusing first year adjusting to university life. He had always done very well in high school, graduating with honors. He was very level-headed and knew that he wanted a degree in computer science. I never would've thought that his first year would turn out the way it did. He was feeling somewhat depressed over how the year had gone and he didn't yet have a job for the summer, which was why he was sleeping in that morning.

Joey, age 14 was getting ready for school. He was in grade nine, his first year in high school. He had always excelled in school and loved sports. He was small for his age and was diagnosed with a growth disorder. According to the growth plates that were done, he was about two and a half years behind in his growth. His small size was deceiving though, because he was strong and fast. He played hockey, soccer and football and he was very good in all sports.

Stacey, age 13 was in grade eight, her last year in elementary school. She was getting ready to go on a three day camping trip with the school, which she was very excited about. She had fundraised to pay for the cost of the trip and she just needed a little spending money. I think she had about $3.00 of her own for spending money but I wanted to give her a little bit more as I recall counting out my change. I can also recall my mom giving Stacey some of her spare change. My mom and dad's house was attached to ours by a breezeway and we were very close to each other...both physically and emotionally. We moved out of Winnipeg to live in the country in 1989 and my mom and dad moved out here too. Bob built them a small house and attached it to ours with a breezeway. This would enable my dad to retire without having to worry about rent or mortgage payments. It worked out really well for both them and us. They were here for us whenever we needed them and we were there for them whenever they needed us. We all shared a very special bond and the closeness that my kids shared with their grandparents was insurmountable.

Bob left for work about 8:00am and five minutes later, Stacey started loading all of her camping gear in the family's Ford Aerostar. Normally the kids took the school bus, but since Stacey had all of her camping gear I was going to drop them off on my way to work. By 8:15am we were ready to go. I expected the usual argument when we got out to the van over whose turn it was to ride in the front seat. Instead, Stacey looked at Joey and cheerfully said, "You can sit in the front Joey".

I pulled out of the driveway and started driving down our road when I got a really weird feeling. I can't really explain it but for some reason I pulled over and stopped. I turned around and started staring at Stacey.

She said, "What Mom…what are you looking at?"

I said, "Just looking at you Stace…I'm going to miss you when you are gone."

She smiled and said, "I know Mom, I'm going to miss you too." I meant that I was going to miss her while she was away at camp. If I had only known!

I started driving again and remarked that I didn't think it would be warm enough for them to go swimming. Stacey said that she hoped it didn't rain the whole time because she wanted to be able to wear the new bathing suit that she had bought herself. Then we were at the intersection. The same intersection that I had crossed thousands of times before without incident. I had to cross the TransCanada, which is a divided highway. I stopped at the stop sign and proceeded to the middle of the intersection when it was safe to do so. There is a yield sign in the middle of the intersection and I stopped and looked towards the oncoming traffic but did not see anything coming. If I had only got there a few seconds later…or waited a few seconds more. I would have spotted the truck in my blind spot. As I moved ahead so did it, so it stayed in my blind spot. I didn't see it until a second or two before the crash.

Horrific sounds. That's the first thing I remember when I came to briefly. There were voices and banging sounds. The voices were the people that were there trying to rescue us and the banging was them trying to get us out of the vehicle. I wasn't conscious enough to see anything but I remember being totally confused and bewildered.

Apparently, the driver of the truck that we collided with thought that he should try to get us out of the vehicle. The only one he was able to get out was Joey. I don't know what he was thinking when he laid Joey in the watery ditch but I assume he was just trying to get him a safe distance from the vehicle. The next passer-by who stopped to lend assistance was a 17 year old girl who had recently taken a first aid course. She saw Joey in the ditch with water in and she didn't want to move him anymore than he had already been moved so she knelt in front of him and held his head out of the water.

Stacey and I were removed from the vehicle using the Jaws of Life. I think that I heard my parent's voices there while they were getting us into the ambulance. The next thing I remember was when I came to briefly in the Ste. Anne Hospital. The doctor was stitching my head which had been spilt open from the front of the forehead all the way back. I don't remember if I felt pain then or not. What I do remember is someone (I believe it was my mom) asking about Stacey and the nurse answering that Stacey was in God's hands. I was thinking NO! This can't be happening.

Due to the severity of our injuries they had to transfer us to the Health Science Centre in Winnipeg. I can remember coming to briefly in the ambulance and they were telling me what was happening. I had taken my nurses training at that hospital and I was therefore familiar with it. It was a very old hospital but they had the latest technology. However, it was also a very busy hospital and was often short-staffed. Would they be able to fix my princess? The words of a Leann Rimes song started flashing through my mind…"If I had to live without you, what kind of life would that be"….NO…why am I thinking that? …she's gonna pull through…she has to!

Joey had a head injury, as did Stacey and I. However, he also had a very badly fractured leg which needed immediate surgery. There was some speculation that he might lose his leg and that was pretty scary. Infection was a big concern because of his open wounds in the dirty ditch water.

Stacey was intubated at the scene of the accident. Her head injury was the biggest concern as it was very serious. At that point in time she had a score of 3/15 on the Glascow Coma Scale and her pupils were fixed and dilated. She had a massive scalp laceration right through to the bone and she had decerebrating movements of the upper extremities. Decerebrating is the rigidity and posturing that a brain damaged person exhibits in response to painful stimuli. The person exhibits extension, internal rotation, and wrist flexion in the upper extremities, and extension internal rotation and plantar flexion of the lower extremities. The jaw may be clenched and the neck hyper-extended. Decerebrating usually indicates the presence of a lesion in the midbrain and pons. On route to the Health Science Centre in Winnipeg, Stacey had a sudden drop in blood pressure which required fluid resuscitation plus two units of packed red blood cells.

Upon arrival to the Health Science Centre, the trauma team had assessed Stacey for other abnormalities; however, the neurological concerns took priority and she went to the operating room directly after CT scanning. When she arrived in the operating room her Glascow Coma Scale was 5/11. Her pupils were still fixed and dilated; she had a corneal reflux on the right and no gag reflex. She had an open left femur fracture and the CT scan demonstrated a fracture through the spleen and liver; however, no free fluid was present in the peritoneum. The surgical team planned to do a craniotomy and evacuation of the acute subdural hematoma.

I don't have a good memory since the accident and at the time I was unconscious myself; so in order to accurately depict the severity of Stacey's injuries I am referring to my copy of Stacey's chart from the hospital. Because of this, this will probably be the most difficult chapter for me to write. As I read each entry in the chart I can't help but visualize and at the same time I feel a tremendous amount of guilt since I was the one that was driving. Over and over I hear people say, "it's not your fault, that's why they call it an accident".

I still feel like it was my fault. Even the insurance company who claims that we have "No Fault" insurance in Manitoba said that it is one hundred percent fault; so how could it not be? People also say, "it could have happened to anyon but it didn't happen to anyone, it happened to me … I was the one driving.

I will spare you all the surgical details but Stacey remained stable throughout the operation. The blood clot was found and evacuated. Irrigation was used to ensure that the entire subdural clot had been removed. An intracranial pressure monitor along with a shunt and drain were then put in place. At the end of the operation, intracranial pressure was 17 with a good wave form. Normal intracranial pressure is 0 – 15 mm HG so to me, that appears promising. Also, her pupils had decreased in size and were reacting to light. That was at 1600 hrs (4:00pm).

I had become hemodynamically unstable because my blood pressure kept dropping to very low levels. Besides multiple abrasions and hematomas, I had fractures in the pelvis, scapula, clavicle and ribs. I also had rhabdomyolosis, and anemia brought on by the blood loss. Upon admission I was started on trauma cocktails and infused with one unit of packed red blood cells. I was given Morphine, Gravol and Calcium Gluconate as well as Phosphate. I was also on C-Spine precautions due to a ligamentous injury to C4 & C5 and therefore I had to wear a neck collar and could only be log rolled. I drifted in an out of consciousness and since I can't rely on my memory, I am now referring to my copy of the hospital chart.

It was 22:00 hrs on May 27 when the Pediatric Intensive Care Unit (PICU) called to the unit where I was to say that Stacey's prognosis was poor and she might not make it through the night. I was brought to see Stacey in the PICU. Joey was brought there on a stretcher as well. Bob, my parents, concerned family members and friends were there too. She was unresponsive and on a ventilator. I cannot remember what was all said and done there but I do remember begging Stacey not to die and telling her how sorry I was. I don't know if she could hear me but they say that the hearing is the last thing to go. We were all begging her not to die and telling her how much we needed and loved her. We were doing what came natural and reacting with our hearts. Now, six years later, I wonder if what we did was the wrong thing. Maybe all that stimulation contributed to the rise in her intracranial pressure. Recently I saw a medical show with a top neurosurgeon discussing head injuries. He does not allow family members to do what we did because he says that the stimulation causes the intracranial pressure to increase. I was devastated upon hearing this. What if this is true? What if we hadn't done that, could Stacey have been saved?

CHAPTER TWO

SAYING GOODBYE

After seeing Stacey in the PICU, the doctor told us that despite everything they tried her intracranial pressure had continued to rise. When we were there her intracranial pressure was 40 mm HG. He said that she was most likely brain dead. I didn't want to hear that…it couldn't be true! No parent should ever have to hear those words about their child. She's going to get better I kept telling myself. The doctor said that they would do a brain perfusion study in the morning but given the way that Stacey's condition was deteriorating it did not look good. I was hearing what he was saying but I couldn't and wouldn't accept it. She was going to come out of this …she had to. She heard us all pleading with her and telling her how much we needed her so she would respond …at least that is what I hoped.

I was told that many people were praying for Stacey. I, myself, am not a religious person but I found myself desperately bargaining …please let Stacey live and take me instead …please.

The next morning at 11:00am, I was taken to nuclear medicine to be with Stacey before the brain perfusion study. Bob was not holding much hope because her intracranial pressures were now in the high 70's. I think that I was mostly in a drug - induced sleepiness then, but I remember hearing Bob talk to the organ donor coordinator and becoming consciously aware of what they were talking about. For some reason I was able to focus in on what they were saying and I opened my eyes and said, "Stacey would want that…she always wanted to help people." I did, however, stress that was only "IF" she was declared brain dead. Then I closed my eyes and drifted off again. To this day, I don't know how I was able to focus in on that, respond, and then drift off again. It's pretty weird how a person can be so out of it and yet lucidly respond to a very important issue and then drift off again…don't you think?

While I was out of it, poor Bob had to deal with everything. It must have been so difficult for him…trying to divide his time between being with me, being with Joey, and being with Stacey. And there were so many decisions to be made …very difficult ones. Thank goodness that we had a loving and caring family there to support him. He discussed the organ donation with my parents and the rest of my family. After that he told the organ donor coordinator that in the event that Stacey was declared brain dead, he would consent to organ donation. Believe it or not, it was something that our family had discussed and we knew that is what Stacey would have wanted. I don't really remember when we had discussed it as a family … I just remember that we did. We actually found out later that even Stacey's friends knew that's what she would have wanted. Apparently, even thirteen year old girls discuss those things.

When the brain perfusion study was complete I got my hopes up. It showed uptake in the posterior fossa and therefore did not fulfill the nuclear medicine diagnosis of brain death. Yes, she is going to get better I thought! However, the doctor was not optimistic… quite the opposite in fact. He said that she had all the signs of clinical brain death. They had done the apnea test and after six minutes she did not make any attempt at breathing. They had also done a cold caloric test to which she did not respond. For that test they flush ice water into the ear and even if the person is unconscious there should be some kind of response because it is quite painful. They could not test for dolls eye because of a possible C-spine fraction. However, she had no cough or gag reflex and there was no response to deep pain stimuli. He said that they would repeat all of the tests again the next morning if she remained hemodynamically stable. He stressed that if she became hemodynamically unstable it would affect her ability to become an organ donor. I think that even then, as distraught and confused as I was, I wondered if they weren't in a hurry to declare her brain dead so that she could be an organ donor before she became hemodynamically unstable. In fact, I do remember saying something to Bob about it but Bob was sure that they were doing everything possible. He said that's why they are going to redo all the tests again tomorrow, because they want to be doubly sure.

All of the tests were repeated the next morning and despite all of the best efforts of everyone involved, Stacey was declared brain dead on May 29, 1998 at 12:45 pm.

Joey and I were brought from our hospital wards to say goodbye to Stacey. Bob, Cory, my parents, and other family members were there as well. The hospital chaplain was there and a small memorial service was held at the bedside.

Shortly after Stacey was declared brain dead I crashed, going into Acute Respiratory Distress Syndrome. A "99" was called and I was resuscitated. Then I was intubated, sedated, ventilated, and paralyzed. They called it type 2 respiratory failure. Apparently I was fighting the ventilator which was why they sedated and paralyzed me.

I can only imagine what Bob and the rest of my family must have been going through. They had just lost Stacey and now it was looking like they could lose me too. For the next four hours things were not looking good. They wrote in the chart that I had been on a PCA (patient controlled analgesia) pump of morphine sage but that I had not been using it. They wrote that I was very stoic and had poor pain control. I was tachycardic with a heart rate of 130-150 per minute and was having very frequent unifocal PVCs (premature ventricular contractions).

Meanwhile, Stacey was going to the O.R. for harvesting of organs. Her liver was going to London, Ontario and would end up saving the life of a 67 year old gentleman. Her heart was going to Toronto, Ontario and would save the life of a three year old girl. One kidney went to a six year old girl from Manitoba and the other one went to an eight year old girl, also from Manitoba. Both eyes were removed and two recipients would each get one eye.

I am glad that we did the organ donation and knowing the difference it has made to each of the recipients has helped us tremendously in our healing. However, one chart entry sticks out in my mind and I will forever remember it.

It read, "eye sockets packed with gauze". I remember visualizing Stacey lying there on the table with her eyes...her beautiful eyes removed and the hollow sockets being stuffed with gauze. I first read that about five years ago in the office of my neuro-psychologist and to this day I still visualize that. You see, I couldn't remember anything and I had so many questions so I insisted on having a copy of the chart...so that I could remember. My neuropsycholigist finally agreed to it but it was conditional. He would request the copy of the chart but we would go over it together in his office before I could take it home. It was not a mistake for me to review the chart though. I had to. If I had to do it over again I would still insist on reading the chart. The nurse and the mother in me just had to know. This might not be the right thing to do for some people but for me it was. The whole time in the hospital was just a blur to me. I just had so many questions that needed answering and I guess that I wanted to be sure that everything that could have been done for Stacey was done.

CHAPTER THREE

STACEY'S FUNERAL

Over the course of the next few days my condition stabilized and they started weaning me from the ventilator on June 1st. There was still an increased heart rate due to sinus tachycardia and the occasional PVCs but things were looking better. My blood pressure was still on the high side so they were continuing to give me lasix and because I was anemic they were giving me packed red blood cells. Oh yeah, that's also when they converted the NG (nasogastric) tube into a tube feed and started those wicked tube feedings. I was very confused and kept asking where Stacey was. Most of the time I knew who I was but there were many times that I didn't know where I was or why I was there. Also, they tell me that I did a lot of hallucinating. Morphine will do that to you.

Since things seemed to be improving they transferred me from the ICU to the step down unit on June 2nd. On the transfer note in the chart they wrote that I was confused and was talking with people that weren't in the room. They also wrote that I thought I was in the hospital in North Battleford, Saskatchewan. I don't know why I thought I was there but that is where my aunt lives and my grandparents lived there when they were still alive. I used to go there when I was a kid and spend summers with them. I was still having sinus tachycardia and my respiration rate was 36 on arrival to the step down unit. Normal respiration rates are 12-20 per minute so 36 was pretty high. I was however, off the ventilator at this point in time.

June 3rd was the day of Stacey's funeral service. They were holding it in the Annie Bond room, right across the street from the Health Science Centre. Two registered nurses and my husband Bob brought me there on a stretcher. They tell me that I insisted on going to the funeral, although I now have virtually no recollection of the service. I remember that there were a lot of people and that Ste. Anne Elementary School (where Stacey attended) brought all the kids there by school bus. I thought that was really special and I know that Stacey would have liked that. I wish I could remember more but I can't. My sister, Maureen Sullivan gave the eulogy, one of Stacey's teachers and three of Stacey's best friends spoke of her. My sister-in-law from Thompson, Manitoba also spoke about Stacey and read a poem called "Footprints in the Sand". My brother Kevin Smith, and my nephew John Sullivan, selected the music for the service and they did a wonderful job. Stacey would most definitely have approved of their selection. The hospital chaplain was very involved in planning the service and without him we would have been lost. He provided a great deal of support to our entire family and we were very grateful to have such a warm and caring person assisting us in our time of need. Our dear friends, Matt and Elaine Kotowicz, took care of the lunch for the service. They are both very special people and I hope they know how much we appreciated all of their help. Our son Joey grew up with their son Lee and over the years and through hockey we developed a very special friendship. There's a lot that I don't remember, but I do remember Matt coming to the Health Science Centre every day after work to see me.

There were many relatives that came a long way for the funeral and to show their love and support at the hospital. There were also many friends and people from our community who came to show their support and we are grateful to them all. Even the mayor of Ste. Anne and the MLA (member of legislative assembly) came to the service. There were many beautiful flower arrangements, mostly daisies, since that was Stacey's favourite flower. She loved daisies so much that her friends nicknamed her "Daisy". Stacey was involved with figure skating and the Canadian Figure Skating Association sent a beautiful arrangement in a figure skate. From what I have heard and saw about the funeral service I think it was truly a beautiful service and I'm sure that Stacey was smiling down on everyone as she watched from above.

On the next few pages there are some pictures from the service as well as a copy of the eulogy that my sister.

STACEY LEANNE PCHAJEK

It is a great honour for me to speak on the celebration of Stacey's life; as well one of my biggest thrills was to be Stacey's Aunt.

I recall the very day stacey was born and what joy she brought to Doreen and Bob as well as the rest of the family; at last I had a niece.

As Stacey grew she was more and more like Doreen when she was a little girl.

Stacey started Highland dancing when she was 3 years old, much to the delight of her grandfather. She entered many competitions and Highland games.

Stacey moved to Ste. Anne when she was 4 years old. There she enrolled in Sparks and Brownie's. She was active in swimming, soccer and even once she was dressed in Joey's hockey equipment and played hockey in Joe's place and even the coaches didn't know it was Stacey. Stacey was a very talented Figure Skater and shone as a member of the Ste. Anne Figure Skating Club.

Once on a family fishing trip Stacey caught a Pickerel that was bigger than her Dad ever caught ... with her Snoopy fishing rod.

Stacey was a great lover of animals - she once owned a ferret named Norton, that was given to her by one of her teachers, Mrs. Dorge. I remember how I use to tease Stacey about taking Norton home to Moose Jaw with me, of course Stacey would always say, "no!! you can't take Norton!" My Mother, Stacey's grandmother used to say, "how can you hold him Maureen, he sinks so much!" Stacey would say, "no he does't Aunty Maureen, I put poweder and perfume on him.....Kiss him Aunty Maureen."

Stacey liked to visit her Aunt Colleen on her farm and ride her horse.

Stacey loved yound children and had a way with them that she could entertain them for hours. She had obtained her babysitting certificate last year and held many babysitting jobs.

To stacey friendship was a priceless gift that couldn't be bought or sold and having good friends and a bond between them meant more to her than anything. Not only were her friends important to her but her family was #1. She shared a special bond between her two brothers Cory and Joey. To Stacey her mother and father were the greatest parents one could ever have and this is relected in these two poems written by Stacey.

MOM

Nowhere could I find a more greater Mom
Than a Mom who's reliable and dear
A Mom who's there when I shed a tear
and when I need a new dress or jeans to boot
Or maybe just a ride some where
She's there to help, always
So where could I find a more greater mom than mine.
Nowhere!

DAD

My dad is hardworking and funny and caring, and
Helpful and there when I need him
If I've ever needed a ride to Brownie's or Skating
My dad would be there or just a little help with my
homework
My dad would be there, so let me just say when I'm
Stuck in a jam Dad would be there.

Stacey was a bubbly, happy person who always brought sunshine into the lives of those who knew her. She loved to be outdoors and loved the sunshine. Stacey loved flowers with the daisy being her favorite, followed by the sunflower.

Whenever you see a bunch of daisies or get a whiff of their sweet scent on a warm summer's day think of our Stacey! Stacey was also a collector of teddy bears and had a great love for them.....so when you hug a teddy bear think of Stacey. Stacey was our bright light so when you look into the sky at night and see a bright star twinkling, think of Stacey.
I feel great sadness over the loss of Stacey but I know she didn't have to make the journey alone and with this thought I would like to read you a poem called "Footprints in the Sand".

One night I dreamed I was walking along the beach with the Lord. Scenes from my life flashed across the sky. In each I noticed footprints in the sand. Sometimes there were two sets of footprints; other times there were only one. During the low period of my life I could see only one set of footprints, so I said, "You promised me, Lord, that you would walk with me always. Why, when I needed you most; you have not been there for me?"

The Lord replied, "My precious, precious child, I love you and would never leave you. During your times of trial and suffering, when you see only one set of footprints, it was then I carried you."

God Bless You   STACEY

Stacey Leanne

It was May 27, nineteen hundred – ninety eight
A phone call at work, to tell me of your fate
A terrible accident three people were in
This is were my sorrows begin

To see you lying so silent & still
How could this really be God's Will?
We all took turns to be by your side
The hospital rules we did not abide

Long hours at the hospital made us all weary
The weather outside had turned cold and dreary
I prayed for you dearly with all my might
But May 29th, you gave up your fight

Your organs they decided to children to give
Your kind heart has helped a 3 year old to live
Right up to the end you kept on giving & giving
Six people have now Quality in the lives they are living

Since you've been gone my tears keep falling
Your precious name, I keep calling
Each day I wake up my first thoughts are of you
It hurts so much to feel this blue!

For 13 years you were my precious niece
Now you are gone to lay in peace
My heart is aching with sorrow and pain
Some day I will come to be with you again
But until then you know how I feel
Maybe someday my heartache will heal

Stacey we love you & miss seeing your face
Your presence in heaven has made it a better place
God Bless you Stacey, please take care
Good-bye are words my lips cannot bare
So I will just say 'See You Some Day'
And hopefully you will Show me the way.

Love
Auntie Colleen
7/9/98

CHAPTER FOUR

MY STAY AT HEALTH SCIENCES CENTRE

After the funeral service I became quite confused back on the ward. According to the chart I thought I was eight months pregnant and said that I was told this on admission. I became very tachycardic (very fast heart rate) and my respiration rate increased to 44 breaths per minute. Then all of a sudden I crashed and a "99" was called. The resuscitation team gave me Narcan because they thought that I may have had a narcotic overdose. After the "99" I was sent back up to ICU for awhile.

It turned out that the reason I crashed again was "Acute respiratory distress secondary to pulmonary edema/pneumonia." The next day my condition had stabilized and I was sent back down to the step down unit. Most of the next few entries say that I was drowsy and orientated to name only. One entry states: "Patient disoriented, asking for her car to get home, unsure of how she arrived at hospital." Another entry states "Patient restless and agitated, thinks she is in the wrong room". It's no wonder the way they kept moving me around. Another entry talks about the difficulty they were having maintaining my C-spine precautions because patient gets out of alignment when she becomes restless and agitated.

It's June 5, ten days after the accident and two days after the funeral and I'm still reading in the chart "Patient orientated to name & at times place; but also at times she thinks she is at the grocery store and left her kids in the car". Maybe my mind wanted that to be true. It sure would have been better than what really happened.

It wasn't until June 7 that I started to be more oriented to person, place and time. The nurse came and said that she was going to take out the Foley catheter. That really worried me because I didn't know how I was going to be able to get up and go to the bathroom when I could barely move. The fractured pelvis was causing me a lot of pain and although it was just a short walk from the bed to the bathroom I knew how difficult it was going to be. That is when I started to get a little obstinate. You see the tube feedings were causing me to have severe abdominal cramping and therefore I wanted it out. I told her to remove the tube feed instead. She said that she couldn't take it out without a doctor's order and I told her to get on the phone and get one because I wanted it out...NOW! She just kept making excuses why she couldn't get a hold of the doctor ... meanwhile the cramps were getting worse and worse. Finally I said, "Either you take this out of me right now or I'll do it myself." We ended up compromising; she agreed to clamp it off and not put in anymore of the Jevity (the tube feed solution) if I would leave the tube alone and wait for the doctor to assess the situation in the morning. When morning came the doctor agreed to discontinue the tube feeds.

That was also about the time that I really started begging people to take me out for a cigarette. There were times when I asked people to take me for a cigarette earlier but I was really too out of it to be persistent. Now that I was more alert I was becoming quite insistent. In fact, I've been told that I was getting pretty mad at people who came to visit me and then refused to take me for a cigarette. To alleviate some of my distress the hospital was giving me the nicotine patches. That at least helped some.

Pretty much all of the out of town relatives went home after the funeral. Joey was discharged from the hospital the morning of the funeral. They showed my mom how to do the dressing changes and the orthopaedic surgeon would see him on a regular basis as an outpatient. He came with my parents everyday to see me in the hospital and they would take him to the appointments at the same time. Joey and I had always been close but I think this brought us even closer together. We are able to talk and share our feelings with each other and I'm very grateful for that. One day at the hospital while Joey and I were talking, I said to him, "You and Stacey had such a special relationship ...you would have done anything for her and she would have done anything for you." He looked at me with such sadness and replied, "In a way she did, mom." My heart sank because I knew that he was referring to the morning of the accident when Stacey told him to sit in the front seat.

Cory did not like coming to the hospital but he came anyway. I guess that nobody really likes to go to the hospital but I could tell that Cory was very uncomfortable. I know it wasn't that he didn't want to be with me …I think maybe he was afraid because he didn't know how to act. He looked so sad and lonely when he came to visit; he was so distant and so quiet. Beneath the sad and quiet exterior though lay a boy who was filled with so many different emotions. He was angry because he didn't get up right away when my mom called him on the morning of the accident. When he got up they had left without him. He told me later that he was so upset that they left without him that he flew into an uncontrollable rage. He screamed and cried and pounded his fists into a tree in our yard until his fists were sore and bleeding. I'm not certain if he rode his bike or he ran to the intersection but he went there by himself. By the time he got there, all that remained was the bloody wreckage. I can only imagine what he must have been going though. Since this is out in the country and Cory didn't have a vehicle at the time, he had no choice but to go back home and wait for someone to pick him up. The waiting and not knowing what was happening must have been so tormenting for him. All of the immediate family members were at the hospital so Cory didn't get picked up until later in the afternoon of the accident. That was so awful for him and I am so sorry for what he had to go through.

My brother, Kevin and his wife Loretta were very supportive throughout. Kevin was involved with planning the funeral service and he took on the very difficult task of going to the auto compound to remove our personal effects from the blood stained vehicle. He later said how difficult that was for him to do but he knew that it would have been much more difficult for Bob to do. Kevin and Loretta's presence and actions were that of genuine love and caring and I was very grateful to have them in my life.

My sister, Maureen had flown down from Moose Jaw, Saskatchewan on the day of the accident. Maureen was also involved with planning the funeral and she was involved with a memorial service which was held at Stacey's school. The memorial service at the school was really nice as it enabled each of the students to express their thoughts and feelings. The organ donor coordinator was there and she explained to the students about organ donation and told them that Stacey had become a donor. The hospital chaplain who had been so wonderful to our family was there as well to talk to the students. There was also an opportunity for the students to ask questions. I really think that this helped the students to understand and deal with Stacey's death. The students had also made cards and posters that said things that they remembered and liked about Stacey. I still have all the cards, poems and posters that the students made and I will treasure them always.

The love and support that we received from family and friends was overwhelming. I remember my sister, Colleen and her fiancé Kent being there a lot. Kent could not come every day like Colleen because he had a farm to run but their presence was also that of genuine love and caring. My husband's side of the family were also very supportive; especially Darlyne and Fred; Wendy and Butch; Fern and Dave; Irene and Bruce; along with Marion and Perry. I believe it was Bob's sister, Irene who started putting vitamin E oil on the laceration on my head as soon as it started healing. She got everyone doing it and it did wonders. The scar looked really bad there for awhile and they thought for sure I would need plastic surgery. I probably would have, if it hadn't been for the vitamin E oil. Doctors and people in general couldn't believe it months later when they saw how well it had healed.

Judy Reidel was a nurse from respiratory at Health Science Centre and she made it a point to stop in and see me every day. I had met her when Stacey was in Brownies and I was taking my nurses training at Health Science Centre. Since Judy and her husband both worked at Health Science Centre and lived down the road from me, they offered to give me rides to and from the hospital. I hadn't seen them much since finishing my training but when Judy heard about the accident she was there right away offering her love and support. When they started talking about discharging me from the hospital, it was Judy who told the doctors that in her opinion I wasn't ready to go home and that some rehab would be in order before sending me home. They agreed with Judy and she suggested sending me to Bethesda Hospital in Steinbach for the rehab since it was closer to my home and my family doctor could take charge of my rehab. They thought this was a good idea and on June 11 they transferred me to Steinbach.

CHAPTER FIVE

MY STAY IN BETHESDA HOSPITAL

When I got to Steinbach's Bethesda Hospital they were very much in touch with my needs. I had worked there after graduating from nursing until the time of the first accident in 1991 (that was about seven months in total). Anyway, most of them knew me there and they were very kind and supportive. The head nurse gave me a private room and she got me a special mattress since my buttocks were extremely excoriated from being bed ridden for so long. Also, the nurses spent time with me whenever possible. Some talked to me, but mostly they listened.

When my family physician, Dr Gordon Dyck got there to see me I was happy to see him … a doctor that I knew and trusted. Yet at the same time I was ashamed and deeply saddened. I was sitting in the wheelchair and he grabbed a chair and placed it so that he was facing me, held my hands and looked into my eyes. The tears began streaming down my face and there was an unspoken understanding. He is a very special and unique doctor with qualities that you just wouldn't find in any other doctor and I am so grateful to have him in my life.

However, in Steinbach they said that they would not be able to supply the nicotine patches that they were giving me in the Health Science Centre. I don't really understand why one hospital could do it but not the other but that's the way it was. Maybe that was for the best though because ironically enough, it was the urge to go smoke that increased my mobility. I can honestly say that nothing else would have got me up and walking like smoking did. At first I could only go outside to smoke when somebody was there to take me out but people started coming to visit less and the urge to smoke increased.

So, I started using my wheelchair like a walker so that I could go by myself. At first it was very hard and it took me a very long time to get out the front door but I persisted. As time went on it got easier but when I got out I tended to stay out for long periods because it was so hard to make the trek from outside to my room and vice versa.

People continued to send cards and letters expressing their sympathies and Bob would bring them to the hospital to share with me. It was truly wonderful to know how loved Stacey was and to receive so much support from the community. We had also been told about a support group called "Compassionate Friends" and after reading some of their pamphlets we thought that we might try it later when I got home from the hospital. There were still times though when it didn't seem real; like I kept thinking that when I went home I'd call Stacey's name and she'd be there. Deep down though I guess I knew that wasn't going to happen so I was terrified to go home. If I went home and she wasn't there…it would be real.

One day Bob showed up at the hospital with a package that had been couriered to our home. It was from Josten's, the company that does the school portraits. A couple of weeks before the accident they had been at Stacey's school to take the grade eight graduation pictures. When I saw those pictures I was flooded with emotion. They had sent the whole package including the negatives at no charge. What a beautiful thing for them to do! Up until this happened, I didn't really think too much of grade eight graduation. It had seemed silly to me …it was like congratulations, you made it this far. Now I see that I was silly for thinking that way. We need to treasure every moment and every milestone for we know not how long we have. Now I am so thankful that the school does those grade eight graduations and I realize how important it is to embrace every moment and to not sweat the small stuff.

Over the course of my stay at the Health Science Centre and Bethesda Hospital I became quite close with the mother of one of Stacey's best friends. Stacey's friend, Kate Spellen, and her mother, Jan, were there a lot for me during those difficult times. I loved them dearly and I always looked forward to seeing them.

Jan, along with two of my other good friends, Theresa Joe who was the mother of Stacey's best friend, and Vanessa and Rolande Meush another friendship that developed through figure skating, set up a trust fund for the family which many wonderful people donated to. This was a big help because with Bob being self employed we had no income and many expenses. Bob didn't work for an entire month. Obviously he was grieving, but I desperately needed him to be with me at that time and I just don't know what I would've done without him. I ended up staying at Bethesda Hospital for about two weeks and when I came home I was still having a lot of pain and needed a lot of assistance.

On the evening of the grade eight graduation of Stacey's class two of Stacey's best friends, Kate and Amy came by after the ceremony to tell me how it went. That meant a lot to me. They said that it didn't feel right to be graduating without Stacey. They were deeply saddened by the loss of their friend and as a result the ceremony was not happy and joyous like it should have been. I thought yeah, and it's all my fault. I wished that I could turn back the hands of time and undo all the damage that I had done. If only that were possible! We were kind of disappointed though because we got the impression from one of the teachers at the school that they were going to make an award in Stacey's memory but that never happened. Maybe it was just wishful thinking on our part. The girls were telling me about who won the awards and I wondered if Stacey had lived, would she have received the Good Citizenship Award like she had hoped. Stacey's bubbly personality along with the fact that she was a true friend to everyone that knew her helped her to win the Good Citizenship Trophy for the last five consecutive years. I also wondered about the Academic Excellence Award because every year Stacey tried so hard to win that trophy but somebody always managed to beat her by just a little bit. I wondered if she would have succeeded this year, had she not died.

One nice thing that the school did was to plant some flowers in front of the school in Stacey's memory. It was nice the way they did it too because one of the teachers took some of Stacey's best friends to a nursery and had them pick out what they thought that Stacey would like. Stacey loved flowers and she was always asking, "why don't we have a flower garden?' Especially since her and Kate became friends; she would go over to Kate's and Kate's mom, Jan, had some gorgeous flower gardens. About a week before the accident Stacey had brought home a Shasta daisy and planted it in front of our house. The day after Stacey had planted it Bob ran over it with the lawn mower. Stacey was kind of upset about it at the time but Bob apologized, saying that he didn't know it was there. Oddly enough, when Stacey died Bob remembered Stacey standing there with her sad face saying, you ran over my daisy. He told me about this when I came home from the hospital and he showed me the spot where a new daisy had sprouted up from the root of the daisy that she planted. It brought tears to his eyes as he recalled this. Speaking of daisies, one dear friend who heard about Stacey's love for daisies dug up a bunch of her own daisies and brought them over to plant in our yard. We thought that was a really heartfelt gesture and we really appreciated it.

Bob's brother Fred, and his wife Darlyne, did something very special too. They bought an apple tree and planted it in our front yard in Stacey's memory. It also came with the following dedication poem:

The Memory Tree

The wind has blown its last gentle breeze,
And the moment seemed so short,
How do we see past the everlasting pain?
Is this all?
The last breath, so quickly drawn
Is no more,
But...

There is one small comfort that I can see...
It will become my memory tree.

I will with love and tender care
Place a tree in the sun,
Where a gentle breeze can awaken your leaves,
So that when I pass by,
And you beckon me with your sweet fruit,
I will remember,

And you will become my memory tree.
Placed for a reason,
A very special reason,

Her name is Stacey,
Gone now,
But my memory holds her dear.

For Bob, Doreen, Joey and Cory,
And especially for Stacey

We are thinking of you with many tears
On the loss of Stacey
And the pain that your family is going through

Please accept this with the love and compassion it is being
sent with, Fred, Darlyne, T.J., Sean, and Patrick

Joey was exempted from his exams and so he didn't have to worry about returning to school until the fall. That was for the best because physically it would've been very difficult for him to get up and down the stairs at the school and emotionally, he wouldn't have been able to handle going back yet. Joey and Stacey shared a very special bond…they were like twins born a year apart and so Joey was having an extremely difficult time with Stacey's death. At the same time though, he was there for me offering me comfort and support.

CHAPTER SIX

HOME FROM THE HOSPITAL

I remember coming home from the hospital ... I didn't want to come home and find Stacey not there. It was so hard to be in my house without her. At first the only two rooms I went in was the living room at my mom & dad's house and our bedroom. It was so weird coming home ...everything felt different.

Home care had delivered a hospital bed which Bob had set up beside our double bed. I needed the hospital bed because I couldn't lay flat as my chest hurt from the fractured ribs. Also, I had breathing difficulty every time I tried to lie flat. If memory serves me correctly the fractured collarbone and fractured shoulder also played a role in that. The fractured pelvis also prevented me from being horizontal. For a long time I didn't think I'd ever be able to lie flat again. I mostly slept and cried the first few days.

I needed help with everything. People had to dress me, wash me, help me to the bathroom, and help me in and out of bed. Bob helped with some of the care but my mom did most of it. Even my sister, Maureen, took a couple of weeks off of work to come down from Moose Jaw and help out when I got home from the hospital. I remember feeling so small and helpless when they would undress me, sit me in a chair in the bathtub, and wash me. Yeah, I also remember a few times when they were washing the shampoo out of my hair and the water went ice cold...burr! I needed a nurse for some things in the beginning too. There were also a few times that three of my sister-in-laws came over to help out with cleaning and laundry. They even brought food with them so they could make supper. Yeah, in the beginning there was lots of support.

My poor mom though ...can you imagine how that must have

made her feel … to see her daughter in so much pain? I looked ghastly; my five foot two inch frame weighing a meager seventy pounds. People tried to help with the physical pain but there wasn't a darn thing anyone could do about my emotional pain. As bad as the physical pain was, the emotional pain was far worse. I didn't want to be alive …why couldn't Stacey have lived instead of me …it wasn't fair. Why did other people get to watch their kids grow up? Stacey was such a good person …always helping people …why her? Did she have to die so others could live?

This is about the time that we started remembering something strange that happened before the accident. For about two weeks before the accident Stacey was hearing voices. Don't get me wrong, Stacey was very lucid and in no way psychotic. Every night before bed Stacey would take a bath and that is when she would hear the voices. All the voices would do was call her name, over and over. After this happened two nights in a row Stacey got kind of freaked. We thought maybe it was Joey playing tricks on her so I talked to Joey and he denied it. The next night when Stacey went to take her bath we were all together in the family room watching television. Stacey came into the family room after her bath and said, "Mom, Joey was doing it again." I gave Stacey a puzzled look and said, "Stacey, Joey never left the family room." We kept trying to think of some logical explanation but there wasn't any. She continued to hear the voices right up to the end. Some people that I've told this to have said that it was the angels calling Stacey. I wonder if it's true and I wonder if she knew in some part of her subconscious that she was going to die. Did she know when she told Joey to sit in the front seat? Was there a part of me that knew it? What made me pull over on our road that morning?

The next strange thing that happened was a letter that came in the mail just a few days after I got home from the hospital. Apparently, Stacey had entered a poetry contest about a month before her death. She loved to write stories and poems so that part wasn't strange. You see, she usually showed me her stories and poems and normally she would have told me if she entered a contest. I did not recall her telling me about entering a poetry contest. Wait, it gets stranger.

This is the poem that she entered:

Death Be Fallen

Death be fallen on those who mourn
Sorrow be fallen on those who die
Happiness to those who live
Living in darkness is not a life
Living life is such a joy...
Live life so it's worth it
Death to those who agonize
Death be fallen on those who fury

I talked to Stacey's best friends and none of them knew about this either. It is strange enough for a thirteen year old girl to write a poem about death, but a month before her own tragic death? It was almost like this was a message to me because she knew what I'd be like and she didn't want me to live in darkness. Whenever I start slipping into darkness I remember the poem and it gives me that little push to continue on.

After being home for a few days I started going into our family room, as opposed to just going in our bedroom and mom and dad's house. It took me at least a week though before I could go into the other half of our house where the kitchen and the kids bedrooms were. I remember going into Stacey's bedroom for the first time; I could smell her presence. I grabbed some of her clothing that had her scent on them and I fell to the floor sobbing. I guess that I was sobbing pretty loudly because my mom came and led me out of the room.

As it turned out, we had to pack up all of Stacey's belongings much sooner than I would've liked to. I don't know if that was a good thing or a bad thing but it had to be done. You see, when Cory had gone into residence in the fall of 1997, we decided to start doing some renovating in our house. We needed a laundry room because my washer and dryer were right at the back door and so when people came in our back door they were greeted by piles of dirty laundry.

We had planned to build a laundry room where Stacey's bedroom was and move Stacey's bedroom further down. Since Cory was away at university we thought that Stacey could move in Cory's bedroom temporarily. We had hoped to have this completed by the time that Cory came home from university in April of 1998. Of course nothing ever goes as planned and we were nowhere near done by the time Cory came home. This meant that Cory would have to sleep in the spare bedroom at me parent's house.

The problem was that since the accident there were relatives there that needed to use the spare bedroom so Cory was sleeping on the couch. We decided that it wasn't fair for Cory to have to sleep on the couch when there was a bedroom not being used; so as difficult as it was, we packed up all of Stacey's belongings. I couldn't bear to see all of her stuff being packed away and those that were kind enough to pack everything up couldn't bear to watch me and listen to my heart wrenching sobs. So they led me out of the room and told me not to come back in the room until they were finished. They had taken me to my bed, where I cried myself to sleep. They say that everything happens for a reason, so maybe that was meant to happen. Otherwise, I would've kept her room exactly as it was and it probably would've been that much harder for me to move on.

My husband's brother Fred and his wife Darlyne had been wonderfully kind and caring. They were there every step of the way for us and I'm so grateful for all of their love and support. They had planned to go to British Columbia to visit Bob and Fred's sister Irene, and her family in the beginning of July, 1998. They thought that it would do Joey some good to get away so they offered to take him. He got along good with their three boys, who had always kind of looked up to him so he agreed to go. I was somewhat reluctant to let him go but all things considered, letting him go was probably for the best. He still had crutches to deal with and he needed to bring all kinds of water resistant bandages because he had to be careful not to get the wound dirty or wet.

I missed him terribly while he was gone and I worried about him constantly. I could tell by the pictures and the phone calls that he missed us too but I'm sure that it was better than him staying home and watching me cry all the time. In some of the pictures though, he looked so terribly sad. My heart just ached for him because I knew too well the pain that he must've been feeling.

CHAPTER SEVEN

COMPASSIONATE FRIENDS

Bob and I went to a "Compassionate Friends" support group meeting. We had read some of their literature and we thought it might be helpful. We were somewhat apprehensive though when we learned where the meeting was being held. The location was none other than the "Annie Bond Room", where Stacey's service was held. I thought maybe it would be okay; after all, I didn't really have any conscious memory of the service. Bob thought that it would feel strange to be in that room again but he was willing to give it a try because we both thought it might help us.

As it turned out, even though I couldn't really remember the service or what the room looked like, I couldn't stand being in that room. It was awful; the whole time I was there all I could think of was this is where Stacey's service was. I think it was even worse for Bob though, because he did remember the service and what the room looked like.

We both felt very uncomfortable at the meeting and there really wasn't anything about the meeting that we thought of in a positive way. We broke into circles and one at a time each person in the circle was supposed to take a turn at talking about their loss. Everyone else in the circle had to sit quietly and listen to the person talking without responding or consoling; when they were finished they would tap the next person in the circle and then it was that person's turn. Listening to everyone's sad stories and being in the same room where Stacey's service was just made us feel worse and worse.

The next thing I knew I was tapped, so I guess it was my turn to talk. The whole time I was in the circle I sat there crying and when I was tapped I just continued to cry. Everyone sat there waiting for me to talk but I was in my own little world. After about five minutes of me sitting there crying and everyone sitting there staring at me, the lady that seemed to be running things said to me, "If you aren't going to talk then tap the person beside you". Bob and I talked about the meeting on the way home and we both agreed that we felt worse than we did before we went to the meeting. We decided that neither of us wanted to go back.

Don't get me wrong, Compassionate Friends is a wonderful organization and they have helped thousands of people. It wasn't helpful for us though because of the location and because the timing was wrong. We were too fresh in our grieving as it had only been two months since Stacey died.

I knew that the location was probably a big factor for us and then I started wondering why there were no support groups out here in the rural area. When I looked at the newsletter the next month from Compassionate Friends it listed new members and people that had upcoming anniversaries and I could see that there were other people besides us that lived out here and had experienced the loss of a child. By upcoming anniversaries I mean the anniversary of a loved one's death. I have always hated that word used in that context because when you think of an anniversary you think of celebrating and who wants to celebrate their loved ones death?

Anyway, I guess that I continued to use it because I can't think of a better word. It bothered me that there was no support group out here and I began discussing it with my Bob, my parents, and some other people. The general consensus was that there was a definite need for a support group out here. With my nursing background I felt pretty confident that I would be able to run a support group. However, I was still in a lot of physical and emotional pain so this was kind of a goal that I set for myself a little further down the road.

CHAPTER EIGHT

GILBERT'S SYNDROME

Cory got a car and a job which was good. However, things really began to spiral downward for him. Within a three week period, he had two car accidents. One of them was minor but the other one could have been fatal. How he escaped without any serious injury is beyond me but I think that someone must've been looking out for him. We were all getting very concerned about him and I talked to Dr. Dyck about him.

When Cory went to see Dr. Dyck he told him that it was stress related and that he thought each time the accident happened he was over tired because he hadn't been sleeping well. Dr. Dyck sent him for some blood work and the next day his nurse called to say that Cory's bilirubin levels were highly elevated. Dr. Dyck wanted him to go right away to see a liver specialist at Health Science Centre. My mom and dad offered to take Cory there. The worst was going through my mind. Was I going to lose another one of my children?

I called my rehab consultant, Kathy Baldwin, and told her what was happening. Bob was gone somewhere doing something and there was just me and Joey at home ...waiting and wondering what the liver specialist was going to say. I did however call Bob on his cell phone so that he knew what was going on and he was going to get home as quickly as possible. I admired and respected my rehab consultant very much and I first met her after the accident in1991. Manitoba Public Insurance thought it would be best to assign the same adjustor and the same rehab consultant for this accident. This was good because it's definitely easier to deal with familiar faces that you know and trust. I remember seeing Kathy for the first time after the accident. She came to my house; we took one look at each other and we both started crying. She understood how I felt and she knew how deeply I loved my children. I think that to some extent she understood the overwhelming guilt that was consuming me too. Anyway, I called Kathy because she had become a very important support system for me. She allowed me to express my thoughts and feelings and tried to allay my worst fears. She, like Dr. Dyck, has a genuine caring quality that gets you to open up. She is definitely another person that I'm grateful to have in my life.

Later that afternoon my parents and Cory got home from seeing the liver specialist. Cory was diagnosed with "Gilbert's Syndrome" which is not life threatening in itself. It is a liver disorder named after the French Gastroenterologist that discovered it. It is believed to be inherited and is caused by a mutated gene (UDP-glucuronosyltransferase), which leaves those affected with less of the related enzyme (called UGT for short). An enzyme is a chemical substance in your body that causes a chemical reaction to happen. Lack of this particular enzyme, UGT, is the key to what happens in your body and results in the symptoms we can experience.

These symptoms include jaundice. This is when red blood cells release bilirubin into the bloodstream, which the liver should pick up and convert to bile and then get flushed from the body. In Gilbert's Syndrome, without the enzyme needed to do this properly, the bilirubin builds up and can make you yellow. Gilbert's Syndrome is also known by this symptom as "Unconjugated Hyperbilirubinaemia".

There are also toxic reactions where parts of the liver, called "Phase ll Pathways", process certain toxins like pollution, chemical fumes, and chemicals in some drugs. This process, called glucuronidation, has been reported to be 31% slower in people with Gilbert's Syndrome.

When the liver's ability to do the cleansing it was designed to do is impaired, the resulting symptoms are jaundice, nausea, fatigue, shakiness, bowel complaints, vomiting, and brain-fog or difficulty concentrating.

It seems that certain things can make these symptoms worse by placing further stress on the liver. These things are missing meals, lack of sleep, vigorous exercise, illness or stress. We know that Cory had been under significant stress, hadn't been sleeping well, and most likely had been skipping meals so everything seems to fit. That even explains how the accidents could have occurred with the brain-fog or decreased concentration.

The diagnosis helped to alleviate my worst fears but there is still not a lot known about Gilbert's Syndrome and what is known is still somewhat scary. I worry about the liver's decreased ability to detoxify and so I wonder and worry each time that he has to take a medication. I guess that people have to live with it and they need to try to avoid the things that make it worse but some things, like stress, are not always avoidable.

I must say though, this definitely added to my level of guilt. I feel that I'm responsible because I caused the accident which killed Cory's sister and my daughter and that created a high level of stress for him. I was overwhelmed with guilt and I couldn't see a light at the end of the tunnel. I began sinking deeper and deeper into depression.

It's like sinking into a black hole and once you're in there it's so hard to get out. You are lonely, even when you are surrounded by people you feel very much alone. Your emotions go flat and everything feels the same. There are no highs and no lows. No highs because you are just too low to experience any happiness or joy, and no lows because you are already as low as you can get.

The thing is, in a strange sort of way you start becoming comfortable in the hole and when that happens you start to prefer to be alone. I remembered Stacey's poem, but it was so hard and I was so tired. I really wanted to die at this point. I started thinking how easy it would be to end it once and for all. I had enough morphine at home. Then I started thinking what it would do to Joey, and to Cory, and to Bob, and to my parents. I knew there was no way I could ever do that to them.

CHAPTER NINE

MY DAD

Shortly after my coming home from the hospital, my dad began to feel very ill. In July of 1998 he was diagnosed with pancreatic cancer. His health deteriorated very rapidly as the cancer spread very quickly into his liver, lungs and spine. The pain became increasingly worse for him each day and within a matter of just two months he had gone from a virile and vivacious man to a frail and debilitated one. His warm and loving blue eyes were now filled with pain and sadness.

He was seventy-six years old, but one would never have guessed. He had always looked young for his age and he still had a full head of thick, black hair. He was very intelligent and had a very sharp memory. He and I always enjoyed doing the crosswords in the daily newspaper together. Sometimes we each got a paper, both of us trying to finish before the other one. For the most part he was better than I, but it was fun. Of course, that was before the accident; when things were "normal". Dad started trying to get me interested in crosswords again during my rehab in Steinbach but I wasn't interested in anything then; all I could think of then was that I wanted Stacey back.

When I learned that my dad was dying, I was emotionless. It's hard to describe what it's like to be completely void of emotion except that you just feel totally flat and nothing matters. It sounds really bad but I think that if someone had told me that I just won the lottery, I would've had the same reaction. That's what it was like.

My poor mom was now trying to care for her dying husband and her apathetic, disabled daughter. She must have been totally exhausted, both physically and emotionally. I remember that she lost a lot of weight and she looked so tired and worn out. I had no strength or energy to help and there was still so much that I couldn't do for myself. I believed that I should have been more of a support though and because I didn't have the physical or emotional strength my guilt level increased.

My parents were always there for me and now when my dad needed me the most I wasn't able to be there. I also believe that my dad probably had the cancer before he was diagnosed but the stress of the accident just speeded everything up. It broke his heart when Stacey died and it tore him up to see the pain that I was going through. As a nurse, I know that stress does play a key role with cancer and many other disease processes so my theory is entirely possible. So, I guess that I will always hold myself somewhat responsible for my dad's death.

Mom kept dad home as long as she could but it was getting harder and harder to control his pain. He couldn't sleep because of his pain and I couldn't sleep at night for various reasons so he would come over and we'd sit there together. Sometimes we'd talk and share some very meaningful conversations and sometimes we'd just sit there and watch television. I'm glad that we were at least able to share those times alone together because I wasn't able to be there much in any other way.

When it got near the end he was admitted to the hospital for better pain control. My sisters and my brother spent a lot of time with my dad when he was in the hospital. They all took turns staying there with dad to help out with his care. They made sure that there was always a family member there, day and night. I tried to be there as much as I could and even though I wasn't able to be there as much as the others, I think that my dad understood. I had brought Stacey's picture to him and asked him if he wanted to keep it there at the hospital. He began to cry as he embraced the picture and said that she was waiting for him. I cried too and hugged him.

My dad passed away less than six months after Stacey's death, on November 5, 1998. That was definitely the worst year in my life. I was there at the bedside when dad passed away and it was peaceful. I wondered if Stacey was there to greet him.

I wasn't very involved in planning dad's service; my two sisters and my brother pretty much took care of everything. It was a nice service and they had a piper there to play "Amazing Grace". Dad was from Scotland and he used to teach the boys pipe band in his earlier years so I remember thinking that he would have liked that. Then, when the piper was playing he hit a sour note and I could just picture my dad making a sour face as he did when the boys in the pipe band would hit a sour note. There were a lot of people at the service; even my physiotherapist came and I thought that was really nice of her.

Mom was holding up the best she could but it was hard for her; she and dad had been married for fifty-four years. There was also the fact that it hadn't even been six months since she lost her grand-daughter, whom she was very close to. Then there was the depressed and emaciated daughter that she had to look at every day. Strangely enough though, I think it was the fact that she had to take care of me and help run my household that helped her to move on. It gave her a purpose and the drive she needed to keep going.

Once again I started thinking of support groups. I knew there was a need in our rural community and I felt certain that I could make it happen. I began talking seriously about starting a support group; not just for parents who have lost children but for everyone who has lost someone they love.

Then I received a card in the mail from one of the ladies whom I had met at the "Compassionate Friends" meeting. She lived in southeast Manitoba as well and she had written in the card that she hoped to see me at the next meeting and she had put her phone number on the card. So I called her up and told her about my experience at the meeting and explained why it was not helpful for Bob and me. I went on to explain that I wanted to start a support group out here and asked if she'd be interested in helping me. She was pretty interested and so we set a date, time and place to meet and discuss how we would go about doing this.

My brother and his wife thought that it would do Mom good to get away for awhile, considering everything that she had been through in the past few months. So, about a month after my dad died they took her to Edmonton for a week. I knew that mom did need to get away for a bit but I had the most difficult time trying to manage without her. It was awful.

I tried to do things and when I couldn't I became so frustrated and cried and cried. My husband and the boys tried to help me as much as possible but I still needed help with so much! How could mom go away and leave me when I need her so much, I wondered. But at the same time, I knew that she needed to do that for her.

GEORGE WILLIAM SMITH (SCOTTY)

September 17, 1922 – November 5, 1998

CHAPTER TEN

JUST FRIENDS

When I and this other lady got together for our meeting about starting a support group, I told her that I wanted to make the support group in Stacey's memory. She had lost her son in January of 1998 and said that she would like the support group to be in his memory as well. So our first step was to think of a name that would somehow include Stacey and her son.

What we came up with was "Just FriendS Bereavement Support Group". The "J" in "Just" was the first initial of her son's name and the "S" at the end of "FriendS" was for Stacey. We also added a picture of a Ford Mustang in the middle of the "J" and a daisy in the middle of the "S" so that it would be more personal.

Originally though, I wanted to be the one who ran it so that so that it could be like a tribute to Stacey. I had all kinds of ideas and visions of how I thought the support group should be run which were based on my experience and knowledge as a nurse and what I believed would best help people in their grief. I didn't really want a partner, I just wanted someone to help me get it started and run it. That's not the way it turned out though. Somehow we both ended up being founders of the organization and then when we formed the executive I became the chairperson and she became the co-chairperson.

I incorporated the organization and got non-profit status. It wasn't long before I began pouring all my time and energy into the support group. I was still very depressed and was not sleeping well at all but this gave me a purpose or a goal to work towards. Speaking of not sleeping well … my doctor sent me to a sleep clinic at the St. Boniface Hospital in Winnipeg. I'll never forget that doctor's cold and callous attitude. He said to me, "You will never sleep properly until you bring closure to your daughter's death". I thought ... well, that's just not going to happen because I'll NEVER bring "closure" to my daughter's death.

I hated that word "closure" being used in that context. Boxes close; doors close; human emotions simply cannot close. Closure has become a fashionable term used by some therapists and picked up by the media and other well meaning individuals. It refers to the belief that certain events allow a person to put the lid on an emotional crisis and move on; but the fact is, there is no closure to grief and loss. I wanted to cling to the past and I definitely didn't want that part of my life to be over. Shakespeare said, "Everyone can master grief but he that has it".

Telling someone that they need to bring closure to their loved one's death is not helpful and in fact, can be harmful. It can be taken in an accusatory manner, implying that the person is dragging things out. The prospect of closure may be attractive, but it's just not possible. It is true that those who suffer will eventually learn to enjoy themselves again. Life does go on but it will not be like it was before, and we wouldn't want it to be.

While some people may think it is kind to encourage those who mourn to forget and move on, the opposite is true. One of the greatest fears of people that are grieving is that if they let go of their sorrow they will somehow be cut loose from the one who died. I didn't want to have anything to do with anything that would signify "normality" because that would mean that life went on without Stacey. Eventually I learned that life does go on without Stacey; but I had to realize that on my own and in my own time. Human emotions cannot be put neatly into storage and marked "closed".

Most people that I knew were very supportive about me starting the support group; however, there were a couple of people who thought that I should be further along in my grieving before attempting something like this. What did they know? I thought. Besides my nurses training, I had knowledge and experience with crisis intervention and I felt that I had a knack for being able to listen to others and provide support so I was pretty confident that I wasn't making a mistake.

My doctor also thought this was the right thing for me to do; he felt that it would be therapeutic for me and help others at the same time. I recently came across this old Chinese tale that is a pretty good analogy: The tale is about a woman whose son died. In her grief she went to the holy man and said, "What prayers, what magical incantations do you have to bring my son back to life?"

Instead of sending her away or reasoning with her, he said to her, "Fetch me a mustard seed from a home that has never known sorrow. We will use it to drive the sorrow out of your life." The woman set off at once in search of the magical mustard seed. She came first to a splendid mansion, knocked at the door, and said, "I am looking for a home that has never known sorrow. Is this such a place? It is very important to me. They told her, "You've certainly come to the wrong place" and began to describe all the tragic things that had recently befallen them.

The woman said to herself, "Who is better able to help these poor unfortunate people than I, who have had misfortune of my own?" She stayed to comfort them, then went on in her search for a home that had never known sorrow. But whenever she turned, in hovels and in palaces, she found one tale after another of sadness and misfortune. Ultimately, she became so involved in ministering to other people's grief that she forgot about her quest for the magical mustard seed, never realizing that it had in fact driven the sorrow from her life. (Author Unknown)

Things were going pretty good with the support group. I got three more people to be on the executive, we were collecting donations, designing pamphlets and other information, and my sons were making a website. We had our first executive meeting in January of 1999 and we planned to have our first support group meeting in March of 1999.

My co-chairperson and I decided to take turns deciding what the topic of the monthly meeting would be as well as getting a guest speaker. As a means of raising funds to purchase books for our library I decided to do a memory walk which would be held on September 25, 1999. We had also decided to make a banner and some t-shirts with our logo on for Steinbach's Pioneer Days parade which is held on Canada Day every year.

CHAPTER ELEVEN

A VERY SPECIAL LETTER

Sometime shortly after the accident, we found out who one of the organ recipients was. In Canada everything is normally kept in the strictest of confidence but as it turned out my husband works in the flooring industry, as did the little girl's father. Although we did not know them at the time, we knew of them and that they had a little girl who was very sick. A few days after Stacey's death, her dad had come into my husband's flooring store and after expressing his condolences said that he believed that his daughter was one of the organ recipients.

You see, the accident had been in the newspapers and when Stacey died there was another article that was beautifully done by reporter Jason Scott in the Winnipeg Sun. The article talked about how Stacey will live on in others through the organ donation. Her dad had put two and two together and figured that Stacey was his daughter's donor. Just to be sure, he said that he would send a letter through the transplant clinic and if we got it, then we'd know for certain. Well, we did get his letter so we knew.

When I got home from the hospital we began corresponding through email. I learned that this little six year old girl had been sick for the past four years of her life. It was labelled "Nephrotic Syndrome" in the beginning stages and "End Stage Renal Failure" as of February 14, 1997.

That is when she went on peritoneal dialysis at home, six nights a week for ten hours each night. She had been through many, many medical treatments and suffered dangerous illnesses, including meningitis. She was smaller and weaker than most children her age but she had a very strong spirit.

Her mom sent me some pictures of the various stages of her illness; there were pictures of just before the diagnosis right up to and including three weeks post transplant. It helped me and my family tremendously when we were actually able to see the difference that Stacey had made in their lives. The feeling is just indescribable! I wish that everything didn't have to be so secretive because I'd really like to know a little bit more of the other recipients. I do, however, understand the need for confidentiality.

Probably the most special letter that I got was from the little girl herself. She was only six when she wrote it and for those of you who don't remember, it takes a great deal of time and effort to print out a letter when you are just learning to print. Yes, she printed the letter herself on the kind of paper with the lines so that you get the right height to each of the letters.

It truly warmed my heart and brought tears to my eyes as I imagined her sitting there writing that letter. She started off by telling me her name, which I'm not going to say to protect her privacy. The rest of the letter goes like this: "I am six years old. Thank you for my new kidney. It is more fun now than when I had sick kidneys and dialysis. Now I can run, jump, skip, and do somersaults. I can go camping and swimming soon. Thank you for your special gift." While that may seem like a short letter to some people, I know how much time and effort that it must've taken her to write it. I will treasure that letter all the days of my life.

I hope that this special little girl continues to do well and that she will lead a full and happy life. We have received a great deal of comfort knowing that Stacey lives on in other people and we have even been able to see the difference that she has made to some of the people. It's truly amazing!

Sadly though, some families don't discuss organ donation. Canada's organ donation rate ranks in the bottom half of countries in the western world. More than 3500 Canadians are waiting for an organ transplant, and every year nearly 150 of them die waiting. We have some of the best transplant technology in the world, some of the most highly skilled surgeons, some of the most prestigious transplant hospitals, but there are never enough organs available to save enough lives. Too few Canadians decide to become potential organ & tissue donors. Too few Canadians talk about that decision with their families.

Stacey gave the Gift of Life because her family knew that's what she would've wanted…does your family know what you would want? If you think that this sounds like a plug for organ and tissue donation, you are right. I can't stress enough, the value of organ and tissue donation; it's a truly priceless gift.

CHAPTER TWELVE

A YEAR OF PAINFUL "FIRSTS"

Summer couldn't have been over quick enough for me. I used to love summer but that first summer without Stacey I literally hated it when the sun was shining and people were happy. I actually preferred the days when it was cloudy and raining. Maybe that's because it was a better expression of the way I was feeling and I wanted everyone else to feel as gloomy as I did.

As summer comes to an end though, back to school approaches. I cannot begin to tell you how difficult that "first" was for me. Stacey always looked forward to going back to school; there were clothes to buy, school supplies to shop for, and of course seeing the friends that she didn't get to see in the summer. When the school doors open and when the buses roll again, people all across the country visibly proclaim the hopes and dreams that we all have for our children. Bereaved parents, having no immunity to these desires and aspirations, realize once again what can never be. Instead, we watch other children who are filled with excitement and wonder why … why not my child?

The other hard part for me was watching her brother, Joey go off to school by himself. Going back to school was hard for Joey, knowing that Stacey should've been in high school with him that year. He would see her classmates that had been with her each year, but she would not be there. He wondered how the kids and teachers would treat him; sometimes kids and teachers don't know what to say, so they something dumb or they don't say anything at all. For the most part, the kids and teachers treated Joey pretty fair though. He did, however, have some cognitive difficulties due to his brain injury and concentration was especially difficult. He found that he also didn't have the drive and ambition that he once had, which is perfectly understandable. Much to his dismay, he now needed the assistance of a tutor. This was somewhat difficult for him to accept, especially since he was used to everything coming easy to him and being at the top of his class before. He didn't want to be different; he just wanted to be normal. He worried that his friends would make fun of him for having a tutor so he didn't want them to know. I felt so bad for him and I would've given anything to make things the way they should've been, with Stacey alive.

Stacey's Birthday

What do you do for your dead daughter's birthday? I didn't know. All I knew was that I wanted her there with us. None of us knew what to do; we were all just so emotionally mixed up. We had often celebrated Joey's, Stacey's, and my dad's birthdays together because Joey's was September 15, dad's was September 17, and Stacey's was September 19.

So, how could we celebrate Joey's and dad's birthday when we were so devastated over Stacey? My sister Colleen and I both wrote poems that we placed at the intersection along with wreaths. My mom had also put a wreath at the intersection and some of Stacey's friends brought flowers there was well.

I'd like to share with you the poem that my sister wrote as it expresses how we were feeling:

Happy Birthday Stacey

It's September 19, nineteen hundred & ninety-eight
Your birthday, but how do we celebrate?
A wreath of daisies we could sit
In the ditch where two vehicles hit
You would be 14 years old today
But you're not here for us to say
"Happy Birthday, Stacey"
Or would you hear?
Are you far away, or are you near?
Today we should have gifts, cake and cheers
But instead we have emptiness, sorrow and tears
There's no gift for you on this special day

Except from my heart I want to say
"Tonight I will wish upon a star
And say, Happy Birthday Stacey, wherever you are!"

Although it was extremely hard that first year, we made sure that we recognized Joey's and dad's birthday individually. We knew that we had to because dad was ill and as things turned out it was the last birthday that we would celebrate with him. We've learned to deal with it a little better now, after six years but that first year was extraordinarily difficult!

First Thanksgiving

There are many firsts to go through after a loved one dies and Thanksgiving is definitely a difficult one. Our family had always enjoyed the togetherness of Thanksgiving; for it was a time to be thankful for each of our family members. Now there was a very important part of our family missing and my dad was dying so none of us felt very thankful. I suppose we should've been thankful for what we had left but our overwhelming grief was too fresh and it crowded any appreciation of what we had left. We could've been thankful for the friends and family that helped us through our devastating loss and we could've been thankful for the time that we did have Stacey in our lives; but we needed more time to deal with our loss.

First Halloween

Halloween had always been an especially fun time for Stacey. This is when you could pretend to be scary, powerful, mysterious, somebody famous, or anything at all! It was a time filled with excitement and intrigue. Bob and I usually took turns taking the kids out to trick or treat. Usually we drove them from house to house in the rural area but there were a couple of times when they went with their friends in the town of Ste. Anne. Either way, they always had an awesome time. I'll never forget the excitement in her eyes on Halloween or the joy that she got from carving the pumpkins. Let's not forget the candy … who doesn't enjoy devouring all those yummy treats!?!

Now that Stacey is gone though, it's unbelievably difficult watching all the other kids trick or treating.

First Christmas

Then came Christmas of 1998; there were so many mixed emotions. I had recently lost my only daughter and my dad had just died at the beginning of November. I didn't want to celebrate Christmas without Stacey and my dad. I didn't want to decorate, I didn't want the tree up, and I definitely didn't want anything to do with celebrating. Christmas was a very exciting time of year for Stacey. She couldn't wait to decorate and put the tree up. She loved everything about it. Then I remembered the last Christmas … we had always had a star as our treetop, but last Christmas Stacey was very insistent that we should have an angel tree top. We all thought that maybe that was another message from Stacey and then it seemed as though we just had to put the tree up and decorate … for Stacey. I went out and got a bunch of teddy bear ornaments for the tree because Stacey loved teddy bears, and of course angels … lots of angels. Every year now, my tree is decorated with teddy bears and angels.

Even writing out my Christmas cards was hard; I was so used to signing all of our names. How could I not sign Stacey's? What I did was start a new tradition … now, every year when I write out my Christmas cards I ask everyone to light a candle for Stacey, my dad, and for all of our loved ones who have crossed over. I also write that if everyone would light just one little candle, what a brighter world this would be! Mom was having a difficult time and things were pretty hectic for her, so that first year she didn't send out cards.

Another new tradition that I started that first year was to send a card and small gift to each of the organ recipients, just to let them know that we were thinking of them and we are wishing them all the best. That first year I found some Boyds Bear pins that said, "Light a Candle" and that's what I sent out. I thought they were just so appropriate! It's really weird because I don't even have to look for the little gifts for them; it's like the gifts just seem to jump out at me.

Oh yes, and I always include the organ donor co-ordinator as I like her very much and feel a very special connection to her. I think that she appreciates the little gifts too because every year when I go to see her at Christmas time, she is wearing her pin that says, "Light a Candle". I guess that I like to think that she is wearing the pin in memory of Stacey but even if she wears it in memory of all the organ donors … well, that's pretty special too.

None of us really realized it at the time, but all of us in the family bought especially nice gifts for each other that first year. Apparently this is common in families after a tragedy or loss. It's like you want to let each other know how much you love and appreciate having them in your life. You are now totally aware of how fragile life is and you want to let each other know how much you care for them, just in case. People are not really consciously aware of what they are doing or why they are doing it, they just sort of feel compelled I think. Christmas shopping was the absolute pits though!

It seemed that whenever I was in a store I'd hear a song that reminded me of Stacey and I'd start crying. Actually, I cried a lot then. I hated the smiling faces that were singing Christmas Carols at the mall and I hated seeing families together with their children. It sounds crazy, but I almost resented the fact that they still had all their children and I didn't. Why them, and why not me? I think that it was worse though to see parents who had children and they neglected to show them how much they loved and appreciated them. Also, when I saw young kids that were drinking, using drugs, stealing, or vandalizing cars I would think, "why do they get to live and not my Stacey who was so good?" I guess that the unfortunate reality is that bad things happen to good people.

We had some really good neighbours too, that knew neither mom nor I would be doing any Christmas baking that first year so they very thoughtfully brought us trays of dainties. That meant a lot to us knowing we were in their thoughts.

Then there were Stacey's friends … those beautiful girls! I love them like they are my own daughters. Stacey and three of her best friends had made this video tape about a year before the accident. On the tape they took turns pretending to be a talk show host while the others were guests on the show. It was really quite well done for their ages and they even did commercials! Anyway, Stacey and her closest friends always exchanged Christmas gifts each year and I felt like I had to keep that going. So, that first year I made a copy of the tape for each of the girls as part of their Christmas gift. On Christmas morning, the girls used to phone each other and tell each other what they got and stuff like that. Believe it or not, there are a couple of her friends that now phone me on Christmas morning, each and every year! I don't know how long they'll keep it up but I truly love them for it. It means more to me than words can say.

Christmas dinner was very strange without Stacey and my dad. There's like this huge void and no matter what you do you can't fill it. I guess that it does get somewhat easier over time but each year is still difficult. It's been six years for me now and it's still quite difficult. The difficulty isn't just with that particular day either … oh no, the difficulty starts with the build up or anticipation of the event. In fact, the anticipation is worse than the actual day. I wanted time to stand still but of course it doesn't; the day comes whether we want it to or not.

No, coping with the holidays is no easy task. I wish that I could give you a magical formula that would ease the dread, fear, and anxiety but all I can do is tell you that each year will get a little bit easier. If this is your first Christmas since the death of your child, you will probably want to spend it a little bit differently than usual. You need to decide for yourself what you can handle and let your needs be known to other family members. Remember to be honest; don't think that you HAVE to take on your usual responsibilities and "be strong" for everyone else.

You are not the same person that you were last year; a very important part of you is missing and you need to be comforted and waited on. Allow yourself to cry, be sad, and if you need to, leave the room to be alone. Burn a special candle all day on Christmas in memory of your child and ask others to do the same. I burn candles quite often for Stacey, not just at Christmas. It helps me to feel a special closeness to her. Another idea that I heard about is to have everyone place a special thought about your child in his or her Christmas stocking to be read aloud on Christmas day. Whatever you do, I think it is important to start some kind of a new tradition to honour your child and use any support systems that you have such as your spouse, friends, children and support groups.

First Easter

The next first that we had to go through was Easter. It was another exciting time for Stacey. She loved the Easter egg hunts and the family get-togethers. Family and friends were very important to Stacey and she really looked forward to holidays and events where we could all be together. She always got so excited with the anticipation of the event and her expressive personality had a way of making others feel the excitement too. She was just so vivacious and animated that you couldn't help but feel the joy and love that she emanated. So, you can imagine how different Easter was without her. I wrote a poem that expressed how I was missing her at Easter and put it in the paper under memorials. It goes like this:

Happy Easter Stacey

The holidays come and the holidays go
But they are so very empty without you here
It seems so unfair that our princess is gone
Your life was cut short, and we wish it weren't so!

We wish you were here, to see and to touch
We miss your smile, your vibrancy and laughter
We miss your enthusiasm for all that life offered
Your life was cut short, and we wish it weren't so!

The Easter egg hunts that you enjoyed so much
Was as much fun for us as they were for you
The family dinners are no longer the same
Your life was cut short, and we wish it weren't so!

We knew that you'd want to help other people
So your organs live on in six other people
We love you Stacey, with all our hearts
We wish you were here to say, "Happy Easter", but
Your life was cut short, and we wish it weren't so!

From your loving family
Easter, 1999

First Tree of Life Ceremony

Each year the Manitoba Transplant Clinic has a "Tree of Life" ceremony. The first one we went to was in April of 1999. We got to listen to some of the recipient families along with some of the donor families telling of their stories. It was very, powerful, moving, and emotionally charged.

All of the donor families were presented with a beautiful medallion in recognition of their loved one's gift of life. After that we got to place a leaf with Stacey's name on the "Tree of Life". Somebody had taken our picture while we were placing the leaf on the tree and gave us a copy. Recently I had looked at that picture and was taken back at how ghastly I still looked, almost a whole year after the accident!

They now have the "Tree of Life" set up for everyone to see year round at Portage Place shopping centre in downtown Winnipeg. I think it's a nice way to recognize the donors and bring awareness to organ and tissue donation.

We've been to a few more of the ceremonies since that first one and a couple of Stacey's friends have even come with us. Each one that we go to gets a little bit easier but it's still a very emotional experience.

First Mother's Day

Then there was Mother's Day. To me, Mother's Day is a time when mothers should feel proud of their accomplishments raising their children. I did not feel proud at all; instead I felt responsible for my daughter's death. The only thing that I wanted to do that first Mother's Day is wallow in my grief; which is pretty much what I did. Then I heard the story that Dr. Victor Gonzales, a psychiatrist told at a "Compassionate Friends" meeting one evening shortly before Mother's Day.

He told of his parents' loss of their first two children. He spoke of how he and his siblings who came later were forever denied their mother's happiness and joy. She was unable to value what she had left as much as what she had lost. Dr. Gonzales said that he spent a great deal of his childhood trying to make his mother happy, always failing and always feeling there must be something lacking in him.

I thought of Cory and Joey and I didn't want them to feel like that. It was not their fault that their sister had died and they deserved to see me happy. It is a natural thing for bereaved parents to focus in on who is missing, rather than who is left. Because of my grief and guilt, I knew that it would be difficult to be happy, even in the slightest … but I had to try because the surviving family members deserved my love and attention just as much as Stacey did.

The First Anniversary

I guess that the next milestone for us was getting through the first anniversary of Stacey's death. I anticipated that for a very long time before the day actually came. I anticipated two dates though, rather than one; the day of the accident and the day that she died. It was excruciatingly painful. I still wanted to turn back the hands of time and I'm sure that most of you have seen those movies where people actually do go back in time and change what happened … well, as crazy as it sounds I thought that maybe if I went to the intersection on the exact same day and the exact same time, maybe something would happen. I don't know what I really expected to happen, but I do know what I had hoped. I had hoped that I'd at least see her, if even for a moment. Of course, nothing happened though. I sat there in my truck, balling my eyes out while listening to the tape of the songs played at her service. I keep that tape in my truck and I listen to it often, especially when I'm thinking lots of Stacey.

Usually after the day of anticipation has come and gone, you can start to feel a little bit more like normal. However, because Stacey died two days after the accident, I'm still pretty much an emotional wreck until the day that she died has come and gone. I write a poem each year for the anniversary and the first one went like this:

One Year Has Passed

A year has passed since that fateful day
Our wounds are still fresh as the blossoms of May

We long to see you, to hear you, and touch you again
This year has been hard and filled with pain

Everywhere we go, and everything we do
We always think of you

You were always so vibrant, so friendly and warm
So many hopes that can never take form

You touched the hearts of those you met

In ways that nobody will ever forget

You taught us more than you'll ever know
And left us room to understand and grow

Please be patient as we sit and cry
We never knew you were going to die

The memories we have of you
Are going to help to get us through

We love you with all our hearts Stacey
Our princess you will always be!

With much love from Mom, Dad, Cory, Joey and Grandma

We wanted to do something special in Stacey's memory and since Stacey loved flowers so much, we decided to do a flower garden in her memory. Her friends came and helped us dig up a garden and plant flowers at home. Then we decided to make a flower garden at the intersection as well. The first couple of years we had the garden so that it was right on the slope of the ditch, as well as on the bottom of the ditch. We had outlined one with those little white rocks so that it was in the shape of an angel and filled it with daisies.

It turned out that we weren't thinking too well when we did all of that because it turned out to be extremely difficult to haul water and water the flowers that were on the steep slope, not to mention the fact that the water very quickly ran off the slope before being absorbed into the soil. Then the ditch got flooded, as it tended to do and all the flowers that were at the bottom of the ditch were absolutely ruined. We learned the hard way and moved the flower garden to higher ground.

We also kind of went a little crazy decorating the stop sign with flowers, wreaths, teddy bears, etc. However, we were, and still are careful not to obstruct the actual stop sign in any way. We had also set up a trellis in the ground and decorated it full of teddy bears. Stacey's friends helped quite a bit with the flowers at home and the intersection in the beginning but most of them are busy and moving on now.

So, now it's mostly me, mom, and Joey that take care of it. My friend Terri, who was also Stacey's best friend Vanessa's mom, goes there with her lawn mower and cuts the grass around the garden at the intersection. Keeping the intersection looking beautiful for Stacey has become very important to me so I really appreciate Terri's help.

Working on the flower gardens at home and at the intersection has been quite beneficial to me, both physically and emotionally. I started off doing it for Stacey, but I think I'm actually starting to like it.

CHAPTER THIRTEEN

IRRECONCILABLE DIFFERENCES

I knew it was a mistake to take on a partner when I started "Just FriendS", the bereavement support group. There seemed to be a constant power struggle between the two of us. She wanted the group to be run her way, and I wanted the group to be run my way. It was apparent that we both had very different ideas and we were both very stubborn.

As time went on, the friction between us became more and more of a problem. It seemed as though she criticized every single thing I did, and depressed people do not take criticism very well at all.

I had started the support group because it was something good in Stacey's memory. In the beginning it was helping me to help other people so I poured all my time and energy into the group. Actually, it was more than that; I poured my heart and soul into "Just FriendS". I wanted desperately for it to be one of the best support groups ever. However, as the tension built up between the co-chairperson and me, I started becoming very frustrated, angry and bitter.

I found myself at a fork in the road and didn't know which way to go. I didn't want the group to fail because it would be like I was failing Stacey, yet again. Also, one of the main reasons that I started the group was because there was a definite need in the community and I didn't want to fail all of those people in their time of need. However, the stress and frustration due to the irreconcilable differences between me and my co-chairperson was becoming too much for me. The bittersweet disagreements were consuming my every thought.

I cried constantly and days would come and go without any sleep. I was an emotional wreck, on the verge of collapse. I tried to be understood at the executive meetings but it seemed like every time that I gave an inch, I'd lose a mile. In my frustration at one of the executive meetings, I became angry and started lashing out at everyone who was there. Then I picked up my stuff and left; never to return again.

It's not really necessary for me to get into specifics; it's sufficient to say that the straw finally broke the camel's back. I was deeply saddened and truly devastated after resigning from the board at "Just FriendS". I had discussed it with my family and friends though, and we just couldn't see any other alternative. I couldn't continue with the constant criticism and conflict and the group no longer had that special meaning that it once had.

I handed over the books that were part of the "Just FriendS" library to one of the other board members and wondered how long the group would continue to operate with me gone. When I had first started the group I had intended that the group be run continuously on a permanent basis to serve the needs of the community. I didn't think that was going to happen now though.

I kept watching the advertising for the support group to see what they were doing and if they were still operating. They ended up operating for another four years before folding; so it was longer than I originally thought. I wasn't really saddened by it because I had expected it. I think that I had also grieved the loss of it when I left, four years earlier. Besides which, I had moved on to other things.

CHAPTER FOURTEEN

THE YEAR "1999"

Cory ended up working at the job which he got shortly after the accident for just over a year. It was at Loewen Windows in Steinbach, Manitoba. His job involved the manufacturing of windows and he seemed to enjoy it there.

In September of 1999 he went back to university. He had a great deal of difficulty with concentration and attention though. He took the television out of his room to see if that would help, but it didn't. Then he tried studying at the university, which helped a little but not a whole lot. He was getting very frustrated because he wanted to do well, like he did at high school but things just weren't working out. I felt bad for him because he was trying so hard and I could tell that he was getting depressed.

He joined the gym at the university and began working out on a regular basis. I was glad because keeping physically active fosters positive emotional health. He didn't have many friends then and he kept mainly to himself. Besides school and the gym, the only other places he went were to the movies, the mall, and Chapter's Book Store.

Joey got back into football and hockey and kept pretty busy. He had problems with his leg and his back which created some difficulties during sports but not enough difficulty to make him want to quit. He also took the hockey referee course and started refereeing the younger kids in minor hockey.

Joey, like the rest of us, was dealing with the loss of Stacey the best way he knew how. When his cognitive difficulties necessitated the need for a tutor, I worried that Manitoba Public Insurance (MPI) would say that he should give up the sports so that he could devote more time to his studies. I brought this up with the neuropsychologist though and he agreed with me that the sports were vital to Joey's emotional well-being. The sports were an outlet for him and a way for him to deal with the tragic loss that he had endured.

When spring break came, my brother wanted to do something nice for Joey and Cory to help lift their spirits. Since he worked for Air Canada he could get a discount on airline tickets so he thought it would be nice to take them to Calgary for a weekend to see a hockey game. I, Bob, and mom were all for it and so were the boys. I had "Air-miles" that I could use for the hotel room and car rental and my mom offered to pay for the hockey tickets. I think that time away did them some good and I was glad that my brother took them.

Bob coped by keeping busy, that's his way. He has been a pillar of strength to me and without a doubt, he is the most kind, loving, and patient man in the whole world. No where would I ever find a better man than he. In the beginning when I needed him to be, he was there by my side all the time. Gradually he gave me more alone time, but he can always sense when I need him.

My mom has become my best friend, and I truly don't know how I'd ever manage without her. She is a remarkable woman and her encouragement, love, and support has helped me get to where I am today. With the clinical depression and the Fibromyalgia that I suffer from, I lack the energy and motivation to get things done. But mom knows how to motivate me and at the same time she knows my limits.

In the summer of 1999, my niece from Alberta got married. We really couldn't afford to go to the wedding but other family members living in Manitoba were going and Bob's brother, Butch and his wife Wendy asked Cory if he'd like to go with them. Cory accepted their invitation and went with them. He ended up having a pretty good time and I think that he was glad that he went.

There was actually more to it though than us just not being able to afford to go; I still didn't want anything to do with fun or celebrating. Part of me believed that it wouldn't be fair to Stacey, and part of me thought that if we could have fun without Stacey, then it would seem as though we didn't need her.

Even watching Stacey's friends having fun was difficult for me.

Of course it was normal, and they had every right to move on and be happy but I'd look at them and think, "How can they have fun and be happy when Stacey is dead?"

I knew it was wrong for me to think like that, and I felt guilty for thinking like that but I couldn't help it. Then I'd be angry at myself for thinking like that because Stacey would want her friends to be happy, and deep down so did I.

I became quite close even closer than I was before, to Stacey's friends. I saw them quite often in that second year and we did many things together. In fact, I grew very dependent upon their friendship. Meaghan and I began emailing each other every day so even if I didn't see any of her friends on some of the days, I would look forward to reading my email.

There were some of her friends that I just saw every so often but I grew very close to Meaghan, Vanessa, Kate, Amy, and Sarah. I was close to Whitney too, but didn't see her too much since she moved to Calgary, Alberta. We went to the movies together, went shopping, talked on the phone … just all kinds of things. We for sure get together for Stacey's birthday and do something too.

Another thing that happened that year was that I started thinking about all of the unfinished things that I had been delaying … things that we want to do but just never get around to. All of a sudden those things were very important to get done. Pictures. My pictures were a mess! You know how you are really good about taking pictures and putting them in albums with your first baby, and then with the second you get a little lax, and by the time the third comes you are really lax? I started going through the pictures and realized that most of the pictures were Joey and Stacey together; there was hardly any individual ones of them. I guess that's because they were like twins born a year apart and without realizing it I usually had their picture taken together.

Then there was the baby shoes. Cory's were bronzed with his baby picture in the frame, Joey's shoes were bronzed but there was no baby picture in the frame, and Stacey's baby shoes were still sitting in a box marked "Stacey's First Shoes". I decided that I had to get those baby shoes done and I decided that I wanted to make a memory album for each of the kids.

The baby shoes turned out to be a little bit tricky because I wanted them done the same way that Cory and Joey's were and the company that did them had gone out of business. After much searching though, I finally found a place that could do them the same. So now they are all three sitting on the shelf in my family room, complete with their pictures.

Meaghan and Sarah came over a couple of times to help me work on Stacey's memory album. Before I knew it though, the album that I thought would be big enough to hold some memories for each year was full. I ended up making that first album 0-5 years old and the new album would be age 6 and up. It turned out to be a lot more work than I thought and very time consuming, so I'm still working on that second one. I do want to get it done soon though, so I can get the boys done.

It is weird but I keep thinking, "What if something happens to me and theirs never gets done?" But then the rational side of me reminds that crazy part of me that if something were to happen to me and the boys didn't have all of their pictures neatly arranged in albums, that wouldn't be that terrible, would it?

Sometime that year I remembered hearing about a friend that had lost her son in a motor vehicle accident. That had happened a few years before my accident, and although I felt really bad for her I had never bothered to call and tell her how sorry I was. It was shocking to realize that I had been one of those people that didn't know what to say so instead said nothing.

We had met and become friends when we were both courier drivers back in the 1980's. We hadn't seen or spoken to each other in about five years but I realized that I should've called her back then, when I heard about her tragedy. It's funny how you don't realize what it's like to be in those shoes until you actually walk in them.

I decided to call her and she was glad to hear from me. I ended up going to her place for coffee and we shared our stories and cried together. We still don't see each other often, but there is a common bond between us and we understand each other.

I no longer put off calling someone who is going through a difficult situation for lack of not knowing what to say. It doesn't matter if you don't know how to react; what matters is that you let the person know that you care. Most of the time you don't have to say anything, because all we really want is someone to listen.

CHAPTER FIFTEEN

THE YEAR "2000"

There was a lot of hoopla for 2000 because some people decided to declare it the new millennium. It was silly though, because everyone knows that you don't start counting at zero, therefore the new millennium didn't really start until 2001. That was just a little thing that bothered me so I had to bring it up. What bothers me is that we could go down in history as the generation that celebrated the new millennium when there was still one more year to go. Why did our generation do that?

It was also the year of "Y2K" Remember all those people that predicted computer meltdowns? It turned out to be a lot of hype to make money. It scared a lot of people though, that's for sure.

Although it was only a year and a half since Stacey died, this was the third New Year's Day without Stacey. Sounds kind of weird, but that's the way it worked out. It's hard to start yet another year without your child; it's another reminder that life goes on with or without your beautiful child. Just a thought... but maybe that was the real reason behind my bitterness. Maybe I wasn't really as bothered about the millennium and the "Y2K" thing as I was about not having Stacey with us.

I was still having a lot of physical pain and my shoulder was one of the problem areas. My shoulder blade was winged (stuck out) and I had damage to the long thoracic nerve which caused weakness and numbness to the arm. That part I could live with, but the pain was excruciating. We had tried many different things at physiotherapy, including muscle stimulators, trans-electronic nerve stimulators (TENS), exercises and acupuncture.

When I received the steroid injections into the joint, there was some relief but it was short lived. The orthopaedic surgeon then decided that surgery would be my best option. The surgery was performed on February 17, 2000 with positive results. The shoulder and arm will never have the strength, flexibility and range of motion that I had prior to the accident but at least the pain is better.

Another problem area for me was that I was having constant headaches that were sometimes very severe and my vision seemed to be getting progressively worse. I had been on so many medications that could cause this, but at the same time it could've been caused by the head injury. Dr. Dyck then decided to send me to a Neuro-ophthalmologist for further examination. As part of my examination, I had to have a MRI (Magnetic Resonance Imaging) done.

The results of that MRI blew my mind! Actually, it was surprising to my doctor, my rehab consultant, and the neuro-ophthalmologist too. It stated, "there is evidence of a left frontal craniotomy with metallic susceptibility artifact noted within the left frontoparietal area". The neuro-ophthalmologist got this report first and she immediately faxed a letter to Dr. Dyck stating that "I must admit that I was surprised that she had undergone a left frontal craniotomy. Obviously, she does not appear aware of this …" Dr. Dyck was surprised at this too because to our knowledge, I had never undergone a left frontal craniotomy. He called the doctor who performed the scan and after discussing it with him, they decided that it must be a small metal fragment from the accident which showed up on the MRI but not on my CT scans because of the magnification used in MRI's. It was pretty weird though, I tell you. Not too much really became of it though, other than the fact that I got glasses.

To measure the status of my nerve damage I had to go every six months for the first two years to have an EMG done. You see nerves can do some regeneration in the first two years, but after two years any remaining damage that you have is considered permanent. I went for my last one on July 28, 2000 and it showed that my nerve damage was permanent. Of course that didn't really come as a surprise to me as I could tell the way my arm was acting.

Cory turned twenty-one on August 9, 2000 and I wanted it to be special and memorable. He and Joey had been through so much and I wanted them to feel good again. Joey's birthday wasn't until September 15 but I wanted them to do something really fun together, so they could feel alive again. The idea that I got was for the two of them to take a sky-diving course, which would be an all day thing, and then after taking a test they could do their first jump. Some people thought I was nuts and that they could be killed, but you could be killed while crossing the street. Stacey was killed while going from home to the school; you cannot base your life on "what ifs".

They both thought that was the best birthday present they could ever have gotten and they were thoroughly excited when they went. They drove themselves in the morning and called later in the day to let us know what time they'd be jumping. We all went to watch them and it was so thrilling! We also have their jumps on video tape as well as pictures that the sky-diving place took from the plane, while they were jumping. They were both elated and it was so good to see them both so happy. Those are memories that they'll be able to treasure for a lifetime, as will I.

On September 19, 2000 Stacey would've turned sixteen years old. Now that was hard - very hard! That would've and should've been a day of celebration. She would've been able to drive a car but because of me that could never be. She never got to experience high school, or have a boyfriend, or get her first job ... or any of the other things that sixteen year old girls get to do. Thinking of all the things that should have been, but now could never be, hurt so much! Mom, Joey, and I went to the intersection and decorated. We strung up balloons, streamers, and banners.

I remember that we had a very difficult time because it was so windy, but we were determined. I had also bought two rose bushes for her birthday, one for the intersection and one for at home. There are six posts at the intersection, two yield signs and four stop signs and I tied a daisy with a yellow ribbon on every one of them. It wasn't exactly the dream birthday for a sweet sixteen, but it was the best that we could do.

If I am remembering correctly, that was the year that I got a psychic to come to our house and do readings for me and Stacey's friends. Usually we went to a movie or something like that in honour of Stacey's birthday, but this year we wanted to try something different. We were all quite intrigued with the supernatural and were all wondering and hoping that we'd get a message from Stacey.

One thing that was kind of touching was that the girls were all asking the psychic if I'd ever be able to move on and be happy again. We didn't really get a message from Stacey, except that she said that

Stacey was "okay" and that she was with us often. I wondered how a dead person could be "okay" but it seems like that's one of the most often asked questions. People always want to know if their loved one who has crossed over is okay … I sort of understand that, but it still seems strange. The girls had fun and it was an interesting evening.

I have always had an interest in the supernatural, but now since Stacey's death, it was even more intriguing. I was obsessed with watching world renowned psychic John Edward on "Crossing Over" TV. I saw all of these people getting messages from their loved ones who had crossed over and I desperately wanted to get one from Stacey.

Bob and Cory would tell me that it wasn't real and that John Edward and his staff had their ways of finding out information by listening to what you were saying in the audience and that John Edward would fish for information while he was giving your reading. They were typical sceptics. I would respond by asking them, "Even if that were true, what is so wrong with it if people are leaving there feeling better?" Maybe he is phoney, but as far as I could see he was helping people, so I couldn't see the harm. Of course I didn't believe that he was a phoney, though. I still to this day yearn for a reading from him, in hopes of getting a message from Stacey.

I have been to a few local psychics, getting my cards, tea leaves, and palms read. They all say that Stacey is "okay" and that she is with or around us often. But I've never really gotten that special message, which I'd know without a doubt was from Stacey. For that, they'd have to tell me something that only Stacey and I knew.

Cory continued to struggle at university in 2000. He had also started taking Chinese Kung Fu classes at the university that year. He had always liked martial arts and he had previously obtained a black belt in Taekwondo at age fifteen. The Kung fu classes seemed to be working out well for him and he developed a friendship with some of the other participants, as well as the instructor. It was good to see him out socializing more.

Joey also continued to struggle at school but he seemed to be doing quite well with the aid of the tutor. He actually had two different tutors, one for math and one for science. He got along well with both of them and valued their help. Sports were still a big part of his life and Bob and I were both quite involved with his sports. What was different though, was that he was driving now. So we usually didn't go to the practices like before, because he drove himself there. It was nerve wrecking though … now I had to worry about both him and Cory. As soon as it's snowing and blowing, or they are a little bit late getting home, you start worrying and wondering. I don't know if that ever goes away but for me I think it's worse because I've already lost one child so I live in constant fear of losing another.

Bob and I get along well and we love each other very much, but there is a problem. You see, here it is two years after the accident and the last time that we had sex was before the accident. It is not easy to admit this to everyone who'll read this in my book but maybe somebody who is in a similar situation will read this and be able to identify with it. After all, one of the reasons that I decided to write the book was because I thought that it might help others who are in a similar situation.

It's hard to explain why we haven't had sex but it is not so much Bob's problem as it is mine. In other words Bob would love to have a sexual relationship again; it's me that has the hang-up. He has been very patient, kind, and understanding about it and I love him dearly for that. But at the same time I feel a tremendous amount of guilt because I should want to have sex and Bob shouldn't be deprived of it.

I shared these feelings with Dr. Dyck and he asked me if I ever discussed with Bob why I'm unable to have sex. I said, "No, but I think he knows why." Being the wise man that Dr. Dyck is, he said, "Don't assume, Doreen. Talk to him and make sure that he understands where you are coming from." Well I was pretty sure that Bob could read me so well that he knew but I decided to take Dr. Dyck's advice and ask him.

Much to my surprise, when I asked him he didn't really know, he just assumed it was because of pain. I told him that the physical pain was only a small part of it and the thought of having sex just terrified me. I explained that I believed that if we had sex it would signify normality, like things were back to normal and I didn't want things to ever be back to normal without Stacey.

To me, that would mean that we could exist without Stacey and I didn't want that to be true. I did want things to be normal again, but normal included Stacey, if that makes sense. So the normality thing played a major role but there was also the fact that I felt responsible for my daughter's death, so I did not deserve any happiness or pleasure. Stacey could no longer experience any happiness or pleasure and it was my fault; therefore I did not deserve to feel happiness or pleasure either.

To summarize that, basically I felt a tremendous amount of guilt because I was not having sex with my husband but I was terrified to have sex because of the guilt that I would feel for moving on without Stacey. It seemed like a hopeless situation but I did want to work through it. Bob was glad that I talked to him about it and said that he was okay with waiting for me to work things out and whenever I was ready would be fine with him. Now, how's that for a patient, loving, and understanding man?

CHAPTER SIXTEEN

THE YEAR "2001"

I met up with my nephew, Kris in 2001. Our family had lost contact with him and hadn't seen him since he was thirteen, which was six years ago. I hadn't recognized him at first, but I was ecstatic when I realized who he was. He had been a missing piece in our lives for so long and it was so good to see him again. As fate would have it he started working as a teller in the bank we dealt at. Usually we did our banking through the automated teller and online but for some reason I had to go inside the branch that day, and boy was I ever glad that I did!

Every chance I got I went into the bank so I could see him and chat with him. He had grown into such a beautiful person; he was handsome, polite, smart, and so much more. Oh yeah, and he had a girlfriend named Stacey!

Joey worked hard with the tutors and he was going to graduate with honours. He had taken extra credits and therefore he'd graduate with 34.5 credits as opposed to the required 28. He had applied and was accepted for direct entry into the engineering program at the University of Manitoba. In order to be accepted for direct entry, your overall average in pre-calculus, chemistry, and physics could not be lower than eighty percent. We were pretty proud of his accomplishments, and this meant that he also earned himself a thousand dollar entry scholarship to the University of Manitoba.

Both of the boys thought they'd like to go to military college so that they'd be better disciplined and they'd also get help with the financing of their education. In the regular officer training program, they will finance your education but you have to guarantee them two years of service for every one year of post-secondary education that they give you.

After filing all the necessary paperwork, both of the boys went in for testing. During Joey's interview they told him that since he was only seventeen, he should go to university for a year and then reapply. The other thing they told Joey was that his math was weak and yet, math was something he excelled in. He not only took all the Applied Mathematics courses but all of the Pre-Calculus courses as well. He got very high marks in all of them too. Also, he took Advanced Mathematics 45S by correspondence as an extra credit in grade twelve and did well in that too. Later though, he had more testing done at the Neuro-Psychologist's and we learned that although he is advanced in math, he processes the information slower due to his brain injury. Yeah, so if he'd have been allowed extra time he would've done much better at the testing. He was disappointed because he thought that he'd be accepted no problem.

For Cory, they ended up denying his application because of the Gilbert's Syndrome, and because when they tested his blood he was anemic. The anemia came as a surprise because he had just donated blood within the past couple of days and we thought that they usually tested your blood before allowing you to donate. After that Cory had his blood retested by Dr. Dyck and was subsequently put on iron pills. He too, was surprised and disappointed when he learned that he wasn't accepted into the military.

Joey had also tried out for "Team Manitoba" which is the provincial football team. He said that he didn't expect to make any of the cuts; he tried out mainly for the experience and because he thought it would be a good workout. After all, most of the kids were twenty years old and he was just seventeen. Then there was the size factor; Joey was barely 5'4" and weighed 130lbs, at the most.

We were all really surprised when he made the first cut and the second cut. The third and final cut would be made after the "Blue and Gold Game" at the Winnipeg Blue Bombers Stadium. Half of the remaining players that were trying out for the team went on the Blue team and the other half went on the Gold team. It was after that game that he got cut, but he made it a lot further than he or we thought he would. He really valued the experience too; saying that he learned more about football while trying out for the team than he did in all the years that he played football.

Towards the beginning of June, Cory began to feel very ill. He was having stomach pains, and was very pale and weak. He complained of stomach pains which had been increasing in frequency and intensity over the past couple of weeks. When he began having chest pains too, we all started to get very worried. All of the details surrounding this are somewhat fuzzy in my memory, but the end result was that Cory was diagnosed with Crohn's Disease.

He got very ill and lost a lot of weight. When Joey's high school graduation came, Cory was too ill to attend. I was deeply saddened by that because now not only would Joey's sister not be there, but his brother too. I felt that Cory getting Crohn's was my fault too. After all, Cory had been healthy all his life, up until the accident that is. They don't really know what causes Crohn's Disease, but they do know that stress plays a major role. We all know that the accident and Stacey's death caused us all a great deal of stress, so in my mind I caused this too.

I was feeling pretty hopeless and depressed as it didn't seem like things were ever going to get better for our family. There was one bad thing after another. It was like every time things started to look a little brighter something would happen to knock us back down again. In some ways I felt like I was being punished for causing Stacey's death; but if that were true, why were others in my family being punished too?

Joey's graduation was nice, despite all of the negative influences. My sister from Moose Jaw even came down for the graduation and that was real nice. Joey won some awards, another scholarship, and besides getting the diploma of excellence he also received a certificate in "Information Technology".

It was really strange though, because when Cory graduated it was really exciting for me; but with Joey's graduation it was a mixture of emotions. I was happy for him, yet at the same time I was sad that Cory and Stacey could not be there. Also, I was sad because it meant that Joey was growing up and I was another step away from losing him. It was really hard to imagine life without another one of my children. Some people are happy when their children have grown up and moved out of the house; but with me I dreaded it. Maybe it has a lot to do with the fact that I still desperately wanted to live in the past, when Stacey was still alive.

Our 25th wedding anniversary was in June of 2001 too. It was really strange. Stacey had always talked about making a big party for our 25th when it came and I believe that she would have, if she were still alive. Part of me wanted to still celebrate but another part of me didn't. I definitely didn't want to celebrate it enough for me to take the initiative but if somebody else had taken the initiative, I probably would've gone along with it. I think that part of me was sad that nobody took the initiative to do what Stacey had wanted to do for us, but then again, it wouldn't have been the same without Stacey there. Cory, of course was too ill to have done anything and Joey knew that we had so many mixed emotions about it so he decided against planning anything.

It pains me to say that Bob and I still had not resumed a sexual relationship by our twenty-fifth anniversary. Part of me really wanted to for Bob, but the part of me that was terrified won out. There was also the fact that I'd been having a lot of abdominal discomfort and very heavy menstrual bleeding so I didn't really pursue the sex thing with the doctor or anything. I had ovarian cysts and fibroids that were giving me a great deal of difficulty. Once or twice I was admitted to the hospital with severe pain when one of them ruptured. When they decide to rupture the pain can be excruciating!

I continued to be dependent on my mom for physical and emotional support. Bob and the boys were there for me too, but I depended on my mom for a lot. We all grew to depend on my mom for a lot, but that's okay because we were there for her in a lot of ways too. Darlyne and Fred continued to be there and supported us in many ways as well. After the first year you stop hearing from a lot of people; I guess they think you should be over it by then. Thank goodness there are still some that know you'll never be over it.

September of 2001 was Joey's first year at university. Although he could get tutors and be allowed extra time for examinations through Disability Services at the University of Manitoba, there was a huge delay getting all of his records sent over from the Neuro-Psychologist's office, mostly due to miscommunications.

He was also somewhat reluctant to use these special considerations because of his need to be "normal". Because of his reluctance and his insistence that he could do it without special considerations, I never stayed on top of the whole disability thing like I should have. He thought it was like cheating because the other kids didn't get tutors or extra time. It was hard for him to accept the fact that he legitimately needed the help. I guess that it must've been hard for me to accept too because I sure blew it when I helped him select his courses. We made the timetable way to heavy and he was soon overwhelmed and overloaded.

Before I knew it, another holiday season was upon us. I think that was the year that I came across those angels at "Hallmark Card & Gift Shop" in Steinbach, Manitoba. They caught my eye right away, just the way I told you before how the gifts for the organ recipients just seemed to jump out at me. They are made of dough and come with a birthstone and you can get a name written on them. I told the lady who runs the store and her daughter how many I would need and what I needed them for. When I went back to pick them up, I was pleasantly surprised to say the least. You see, the lady that owns and runs the Hallmark store in Steinbach called the lady who owns the company that makes those angels so that she could order the number of angels that I needed. The Hallmark lady ended up telling the lady who makes the angels what I wanted them for and she was so touched that she told the Hallmark lady that she would send them all to me for free! The Hallmark lady, her daughter, my mom, and me were all very touched by that lady's gesture; what a wonderful thing to do! I feel that she deserves a special place in my heart and in my book. The name of her company is "Vincent Van Dough" and her creations are handcrafted in Victoria, British Columbia. If you are ever in a store and see her creations, I hope that you'll remember what a warm and special person that she is.

I think that the anticipated grief over the holiday season was maybe a little bit less intense this year. I saw all of Stacey's friends like I did in the past and I was very grateful that they still thought of me and cared enough to come and spend time with me at Christmas.

Stacey's friends and I continued to have an interest in the supernatural. Meaghan, Sarah, and I started playing around with an Ouija board. We didn't have a clue what we were doing but we desperately wanted to contact Stacey. It started getting really freaky because it started going crazy, all by itself. It was going back and forth, back and forth really fast on the board and we didn't know what to make of it. We called an acquaintance that we thought knew about that kind of stuff, hoping that she could help us. She told us that it was very dangerous to play around with an Ouija board when you didn't know what you were doing. She said that by summoning Stacey through the Ouija board we were asking her to come through where all kinds of evil existed as well. We didn't know that before but now that we did, none of us wanted anymore to do with the Ouija board. The lady that we called understood our desperate need to contact Stacey though, so she offered to come to my house and do a séance.

The day of the séance was eagerly anticipated by us all. There was the lady doing the séance, her daughter, my mom, Kate, Meaghan, Vanessa, and myself. The lady had done quite a few of these séances in the past so she knew what she was doing. We had a circle of protection and she started off with a prayer. Stacey never came through for us that night, but there were a couple of other spirits that did. There were two times that we had to stop because of things that were happening. Once was when my mom and the lady doing the séance (she was sitting next to my mom) felt a really cold draft and somebody was standing over them. They could actually feel him breathing on them and it started to freak even the lady out so she stopped. The other time when we stopped it was like somebody was trying to pull me out of the circle. You see when you are in the circle of protection, everyone has their hands joined and there was some kind of spirit or force that kept trying to break my hold with Vanessa, who was sitting next to me. We were all a little freaked by the end of the evening but at the same time we were disappointed that Stacey never came through.

We haven't done anymore séances since then but we still go to get our tea leaves, cards, or palms read. However, I wouldn't mind doing another séance as I still desperately want to get a message from Stacey.

CHAPTER SEVENTEEN

THE YEAR "2002"

On January 30, 2002, Stacey's friend Vanessa turned sixteen. That was very hard for me because Vanessa was two years younger than Stacey but since Stacey died when she was thirteen, Vanessa had already done more things than Stacey. Things like getting her driver's license, having a boyfriend, having a sweet sixteen birthday, attending the senior prom, were all things that Vanessa had experienced but Stacey would never experience. It's not that I resented Vanessa for experiencing those things; but I resented or hated myself because it was my fault that my daughter would never experience the joys in life that her friends could.

Things were going pretty good with my nephew Kris. We had some nice visits and some good talks. It was so good to have him back in our lives again. His girlfriend Stacey was absolutely adorable and we fell in love with her right away.

Kris and his girlfriend Stacey took a Teaching English as a Second Language (TESOL) course and completed it by the end of 2001. They both went to China to teach English in February of 2002. I was happy for them because I knew it would be a wonderful experience but at the same time I was worried about the two of them going off to a strange country. They had planned to stay for six months to a year but Stacey's mom got ill so they came back a little before the six months were up.

Kris was really thin when he came back and I remember asking him if he didn't like the food there. He explained that he probably ate more there than he did here in Canada but the food was so much healthier and also they walked pretty much everywhere they went as opposed to riding in a vehicle like they would if they were in Canada.

I was glad they were back safe and sound and of course so were their mothers, who worried like crazy while they were gone. They enjoyed the experience immensely and were glad that they had the opportunity.

The first semester was bad enough, but by the second semester of the 2001-02 school year, Joey was really having difficulty. Disability Services finally got all the necessary paperwork and all the special considerations were put into place but we had left it too long and the first year was a total mess. He ended up redoing a couple of the courses during the spring and summer session and he did pretty well with both of them

After we learned more about Disability Services, I told Cory that he should go there and see if there was any way that they could help him with his concentration difficulties and Crohn's Disease. His concentration and ability to focus was getting to be more and more of a problem and as a result he was not doing well with his courses. He decided to take my advice because he wanted to be able to do better and was getting very frustrated and discouraged.

They, at disability services, did all kinds of testing on Cory and in the end they diagnosed him with "Adult Attention Deficit Disorder". Just one more thing to add to his list of difficulties, but at least now he could get help. By the end of the year though, he knew that he would have to drop out of the Faculty of Science. The science courses just seemed to take much more memory, attention and concentration than the arts courses; so he transferred into the Faculty of Arts.

In April of 2002, I had a small stroke. It was very mild and I lost the use of my arm for about a week. During the second and third week I gradually got back more and more use of the arm. The thing that made it most difficult was that it was my good arm that was affected, the one that didn't have the nerve damage and stuff. I believed then, and I believe to this day that it was the "Vioxx" (a cox 2 inhibitor that I was taking for pain) that caused that mini stroke. When all the controversy about Vioxx causing strokes came out in late 2004, I thought, "Yeah, I knew it".

In May of that year my mom turned seventy-five. I wanted to do something special for her that year and since she always enjoyed going to "Temple Gardens Mineral Spa" in Moose Jaw that's what we decided to do. I used my air miles and got two rooms for the weekend, one for me, Bob, Joey and Cory, and the other for my mom, her sister, and her cousin. Since my sister Maureen lived in Moose Jaw, we planned and co-ordinated everything together. It turned out to be a really nice weekend and my mom thoroughly enjoyed herself.

In June of 2002, Stacey would've graduated from high school. I wanted to go to the graduation in support of her friends but I was very apprehensive because I didn't know if I could handle it. Sometimes fate has a way of making the decisions for you though, because as it turned out I ended up in the hospital having a hysterectomy when the graduation occurred. I had gotten gifts for all of her friends that were graduating though and Bob went to the ceremony and videotaped it for me.

Stacey's friend, Amy was valedictorian and she talked about Stacey in her speech. It was a very heartfelt speech and Amy was not the only one crying. I don't know if I would've been able to handle that without crying hysterically so it's probably good that I wasn't there.

Stacey's friend Kate had joined the military and was going for her basic training that summer. It was kind of weird the way that worked out though because Kate's dad was an army sergeant and he had always told her that if she wanted to go to university, that's the route that she'd have to go. Kate really was never that keen on joining the military so when she told me that she had applied I was quite surprised. Even when she went to apply she was still somewhat apprehensive and yet she was accepted right away. That part kind of bothered me though, because Joey and Cory really wanted to be accepted when they applied to the military but they were not accepted. Kind of weird the way things work out sometimes, isn't it?

In September of 2002, Stacey would've turned 18 and she would've been going to university. This was the fifth birthday that she missed, so you'd think that I'd be handling it okay, but you'd be wrong. It hurt so incredibly much!

This should have been one of the most exciting times in her life but she was dead. How does a parent deal with that? I sat there alone, at the intersection listening to the tape of songs played at her service and I cried my eyes and heart out. Of course we decorated the intersection and I planted flowers in her memory but that doesn't take the hurt away. I went to the florist and got them to make a really big number "1" and a number "8" out of yellow and white daisies and we stuck them in the ground at the intersection so that they were standing upright. I wanted her to know that we were thinking about her and I wondered if she was watching us and smiling.

It was around this time that my brother and his wife located my dad's relatives in England and Scotland. You see my dad was from Scotland and when he met my mom he was in the British Air Force and was stationed in North Battleford, Saskatchewan, where my mom was living. They got married and mom went back to England with him. My oldest sister, Maureen was born in Edinburgh and when Maureen was three years old they decided to move to Canada. Mom and dad stayed in contact with his family for the first while but somehow they lost contact with each other. Dad found out later that his mother had passed away and he was angry that nobody had notified him when it happened. Somehow, after that they all lost contact with each other; until now that is.

My brother and sister were ecstatic, but I really didn't know how to react. I was very close to my dad and all I could remember was how hurt my dad was when they didn't contact him about his mother's death. However, it was also apparent that my dad missed his home and family and maybe there was some kind of logical explanation why they hadn't contacted him.

The first semester in the 2002-03 school year went very well for Joey. He took less courses; at least half of what he attempted the year before and that seemed to work well for him. He got all B's and B+'s so I had my hopes up that he was going on the right track.

Now that Cory was in the faculty of arts, he was doing much better with his courses. He was taking a variety of courses but majored in criminology. He said that he'd one day like to work with youth, in crime prevention. Something else happened to Cory in 2002; he met a girl named Gigi in his Kung-Fu class. She was a very pretty Asian girl with a cute little voice and a very nice smile. The first time that Cory brought her here, she was surprised to see Joey because Joey was in their Kung-Fu class too, but she never realized that they were brothers. They actually do look a lot alike, but it just didn't dawn on her that they were brothers ... I guess that she only had eyes for Cory!

Gigi's parents, along with her brother and sister lived in Vancouver, British Columbia and she planned on going home for the

Christmas break. She asked Cory to go with her and he was only too happy to oblige.

That meant that we'd be spending Christmas not only without Dad and Stacey, but without Cory now too. We decided to try something different and go away for Christmas so we ended up going to Moose Jaw to spend Christmas with my sister and her family. We had never been away from home at Christmas before and I had a very difficult time being away from home this time. We still lit a special candle for Stacey at Maureen's, but it just didn't feel right to be away from home. I was missing Stacey, I was missing Cory, and I was away from my familiar surroundings. Then there was the fact that I wouldn't be home on Christmas morning to talk to Stacey's friends on the phone and that was important to me. I found that Christmas to be extremely difficult and I would caution anyone who is in a similar situation to think twice before breaking from your usual routine during the holiday season.

Things still hadn't changed as far as sex goes with Bob and me. I felt very guilty about that but didn't know what to do. I did think about it a lot but I was afraid … afraid of letting go. I didn't really feel comfortable enough to bring it up for discussion with my psychologist. Actually, I think that I may have brought it up once or twice but then felt so embarrassed and uncomfortable that I just quickly changed the subject. I felt more comfortable discussing things like that with my family doctor but lately he seemed so rushed and busy so the opportunity hadn't presented itself.

I was sure glad that I had the hysterectomy done though. What a relief it was … and is, to be rid of all that pain! Having no more periods was an absolute bonus. Having suffered through years of endometriosis definitely makes one appreciate the benefits of having a hysterectomy. While it might not be the treatment of choice for everyone that suffers from endometriosis, it certainly was the right thing for me.

CHAPTER EIGHTEEN

THE YEAR "2003"

On January 12, 2003 my mom was having severe abdominal pain and I took her to the hospital in Steinbach where she was admitted. They ran many tests trying to find out what the problem was and finally on January 18 they did surgery to relieve and repair a small bowel obstruction.

It was pretty scary while mom was in the hospital and we were really worried about her. She had to be on a lot of medication to control the pain and they were making her drowsy, and at times confused. Then when she had the surgery, the cumulative effects of the anaesthetic, narcotics and her age caused me to be very concerned. She became a totally different person, hallucinating, disoriented, agitated, and confused. There is no question that significant cognitive dysfunction can be found in elderly patients following surgery. In some cases, and to an unknown degree, the anaesthesia has been associated with the acceleration of senile dementia or Alzheimer's disease.

Three days after the surgery she was still experiencing significant cognitive dysfunction. She was very agitated, saying that she couldn't sleep at night because kids were jumping on her bed and a man was peering in her window. She was angry at the nurses because she said that they would laugh at her when she called them to tell them about the kids jumping on her bed and the man peering in her window.

Of course none of this was really happening, but to her it seemed very real. She was insisting that I take her home right now. I tried to explain that she had no clothes there for me to bring her home and that I would come back the next day with clothes to bring her home. However, she was extremely agitated and insisted upon leaving. The nurses called the surgeon and I spoke with him on the phone. After discussing the situation, we both felt that it would be best to take her home and hopefully when she was in her own familiar surroundings she would settle down. So I ended up taking her home in her nightgown, with a blanket wrapped around her in the middle of January. For those of you who don't know, it gets pretty cold here in mid January.

Much to my relief, mom did settle down once she got home in familiar surroundings. It took a few more days for the confusion and disorientation to subside but before long she was back to her loveable self. Thank goodness for that!

In February, my brother and sister, along with their spouses went to England to see my dad's relatives. They were pretty excited about going and had been communicating back and forth with dad's relatives since the fall. Their trip was only for one week, which wasn't a lot of time to see everyone in England and Scotland but they made the most of their time. They brought back many wonderful pictures and memories and they were glad to complete that missing piece in dad's life.

For about the past year, mom was experiencing decreasing vision due to cataracts in both eyes. You just don't realize how valuable your eyesight is until you start losing it. She was on the waiting list for surgery for about six months, before having her first surgery in February of 2003. The results were evident almost immediately; when the doctor took the bandage off the next day it was like a miracle had happened and she could see again! It is amazing what a difference that the surgery made. Mom was thrilled and I was very happy for her. Since you can only have one eye done at a time, she would be put back on the waiting list to have the second eye done.

At the end of April, Joey finished the second semester and completed the 2002-2003 school year. That school year had gone pretty well for him except that he had only taken two courses each semester. That part bothered him because he thought at that rate it would take him forever to complete the engineering program. I guess that it had me a little concerned too because there is a maximum time limit for you to complete the program.

In May of 2003 it was the fifth anniversary since Stacey's death and I marked it in a very special way. I founded and incorporated the "Stacey Pchajek Memorial Foundation Inc.". The foundation is a non-profit, charitable organization providing scholarships, bursaries and prizes to students graduating grades eight and twelve in southeast Manitoba. Education was very important to Stacey so it was only fitting that the foundation be established.

Candidates are nominated by their peers and teachers in the form of an essay stating why that person deserves to win. The recipients should reflect the type of person that Stacey was. Although she was not always the top achiever academically, she consistently put forth her best effort into everything she did. She was a happy, well-rounded individual who was very helpful and supportive to her peers. She was a friend to all and she always looked for the good in things. I developed a set of criteria that include these qualities about Stacey and I hope that it will help students realize that even though you may not be the smartest person at your school, it's important to be a good person and always put forth your best effort.

Stacey's friend Amy is the secretary and my sister-in-law Darlyne is the treasurer for the foundation. It's been a lot of work getting the foundation off the ground, and fundraising is a chore in itself. For the remaining months in 2003 I mainly just collected donations. I planned the first major fundraiser for February of 2004 and it was going to be a "Good Time Oldies" fundraising social.

Stacey's friends came over and helped me design a logo and Joey worked on refining it. We decided on using the yellow ribbon of hope with a daisy on it as part of the logo. The daisy seemed to add the warmth and personality of Stacey. Joey also did a wonderful job designing and implementing a website for the foundation. The website has a picture gallery showing some wonderful memories of Stacey and a video. The video was put together by Stacey's friend Meaghan and it's very well done as well as a very touching and thoughtful gesture of her memories of Stacey. Many wonderful stories and poems can also be found on the forums page.

The foundation has given me a new purpose and goal in life and while it takes up a lot of my time, I am very proud of it and I think Stacey would be too. My family has been very supportive and helpful with regards to the foundation and I love them for it.

We were also very pleased to attend Cory's convocation at the University of Manitoba in May of 2003. We were very proud of all his hard work and determination. While the going definitely got tough for him along the way, he persisted and prevailed. He graduated with a Bachelor of Arts, majoring in Criminology, with a minor in psychology. It was a long, but very nice ceremony. Afterwards, we had a big barbecue to celebrate his graduation with friends and relatives.

Cory and Gigi's relationship was blossoming into true love. It appeared that I was losing my son to this pretty Asian girl, with her tiny voice and her cute little laugh. I thought that I'd be more upset when that happened, but I wasn't. I was okay with it because Cory was happy, and that's all that mattered. Of course, we'd all grown to love Gigi too; she was a warm, loving and caring person and you couldn't help but fall in love with her.

Cory changed in a spiritual way too. Our family had always been agnostic, but in the past year Cory found religion. He began attending church on a regular basis and even going to bible study meetings. We were all very surprised at the changes in him with regards to religion and we wondered how much of a role that Gigi played in it all. He assured us that choosing to have God in his life was his decision and that his relationship with Gigi had in no way influenced his decision. It was all really strange to us because we were actually closer to being atheists than agnostic. Cory took his religion very serious though and he even got baptized in 2003. Can you imagine us agnostic/atheists at a baptism? It was really strange but we felt that we needed to go to show our support to Cory.

Some of you might be thinking poorly of us now, because we are agnostic/atheist. However, we are very good people with excellent morals. We simply choose not to believe in God. Then there are those that say, "If you believe in Angels, you must believe in God." I can't really explain that except to say that is probably the agnostic part of me believing in angels. An agnostic basically says that if you can prove that it's true, then I'll believe it. But an atheist pretty much just denies the existence of God. Anyway, I think that if there is a chance that God exists and there are such things as angels, then I want Stacey to be one. Hopefully, that makes sense to you.

In July mom had her second eye surgery done. We were hoping that it would have the same positive results as the first eye surgery and luckily it did. Mom was thrilled to be able to see clearly again. My sister came down from Moose Jaw to help out as mom needed to take it easy for a few days. She also assisted my mom by putting her eye drops in and helping out with cooking and cleaning.

While Maureen was here, the two of us decided to do something that had interested us for awhile and that involved making willow furniture. There was a place not far from my home that does willow workshops where you learn to make your own chair. The cost of the workshop included your materials and then we'd end up with our own chair. At the workshop though, I encountered a great deal of difficulty due to the impairments in my arm and shoulder. I felt bad because the instructor had to do so much of it for me and that took a lot of time away from her teaching the others what to do. It was very frustrating for me as I tried hard but just didn't have the physical capability that was required. I was grateful that the instructor helped me and we got the chair finished but it wasn't quite the same as if I had done the whole thing myself, like the others.

Cory turned twenty-four on August 9th and marked his birthday by proposing to Gigi. He had planned out a whole romantic scenario but nothing ever goes as planned for our family. Gigi ended up having emergency surgery the day before his birthday and since I knew what Cory's plans were, I asked him if he was still going to propose to Gigi on his birthday, now that she was in the hospital. He wasn't sure at first but I told him that it wasn't important how or where he did it; if he really wanted to ask her then he should just go ahead and do it. So, he proposed on bended knee at the hospital bedside and Gigi accepted. It actually is romantic when you think about it.

In September we had another strange occurrence. It was right around Stacey's birthday and I was working on the flower gardens. As I was digging around the Calla Lilies, right near the top of the ground I found a coin. I looked at the coin and saw that it was an old American fifty cent piece. Since Bob collected old coins, I gave it to him. I didn't really think too much of it but later that night I had a dream.

In the dream, Stacey came to me and said, "I left you the coin to let you know that I'm still around mom. The coin is 1919 because I'll be 19 on the 19." It was so weird that I even had the dream because I rarely ever dream. You see, people with Chronic Fatigue/Fibromyalgia rarely go into REM sleep (when you dream), which is one of the reasons we are so tired all the time.

Anyway, when I woke up Bob of course was gone to work, so I waited for him to get home to ask him about the coin. It had looked old when I saw it, but I never looked at the year. When Bob got home I couldn't wait to ask him about the coin. I said to him, "You know that coin that I gave you yesterday?" He said, "Yeah, what about it?" I then asked him what year it was and he replied matter-of-factly, "1919, why?" I told him about the dream and we were both full of wonder and amazement.

In the fall that year, Cory informed us that Gigi would be graduating by mid December and he planned on moving to B.C. with her. They had talked about living here and having the wedding here for awhile but then changed their mind. The wedding was now going to be held in May of 2004, in Vancouver, B.C.

Because Christmas had been so difficult for me the year before, I really wanted them to stay at least until after Christmas. In fact, I pretty much begged them to stay for Christmas but they had already signed up for a TESOL course in Vancouver that started almost immediately after Gigi's courses ended here. I had to accept the fact that Cory was all grown up now and would be starting a new life.

It was really hard at first when Cory left but we talked to each other almost daily for awhile. Most of the time, we chat on MSN via the internet because it's cheaper than the telephone. Bob even got me a web cam so that Cory and I could see each other while we chat. Yeah, so while Cory has moved on, he's not gone in the way that Stacey is and I'm thankful for that.

I think that Cory's leaving affected Joey in a very big way. He started off the 2003-04 year doing quite well in the first semester but after Cory announced that he'd be leaving, Joey started falling behind in his work. Was it a coincidence? Maybe, but I don't think so. He ended up getting C+'s in all of his courses that first semester, but he had taken five courses. So it could have been that he was overwhelmed and overloaded again, but I think that Cory's leaving also played a role.

We managed to get through Christmas okay. Mom and I didn't have to cook that year as we were invited to Darlyne & Fred's for Christmas dinner. My sister Colleen and Kent were invited as well and we had a very enjoyable dinner. After last year, I thought that I'd never want to have another Christmas away from home but this was different. This time we were still in our own house on Christmas Eve and Christmas morning and we went home later that night. I found that the familiar surroundings were, and are, very important to me.

CHAPTER NINETEEN

THE YEAR "2004"

Joey got severely depressed after Cory left. He got really far behind in his classes and then he just quit going. He was sleeping all day and staying up at night. Days would go by without him even setting foot outside the door. Like I said before, I think part of it was due to him being overloaded and overwhelmed but I think it bothered him more than he himself realized when Cory moved away. It was like losing another sibling and I don't think that he ever really dealt with losing Stacey.

It was really hard to watch him like that; my heart ached for him. He also gained a fair amount of weight due to his inactivity. Not so much that he was obese, but certainly more than he should weigh. I tried to convince him to go to the gym and stuff but he just didn't have the drive or ambition.

He did go to the doctors and was put on antidepressants but depression is a cruel illness and once it has a hold of you it doesn't want to let go. Sometimes the antidepressants don't seem to do anything, but they usually take 3-4 weeks before you start noticing any improvement. Even then, the dosages are usually increased at least a couple of times. Then, if there is still no improvement, they'll try you on a different kind. Sometimes too, one drug might work for a while on you and that quit working. Quite often when you are suffering from depression you are put on two different types because one drug helps to increase the efficiency of the other. He's already been on a few different kinds; I have been on many. One thing is for certain though, and that is the fact that I would not be able to function without my antidepressants. I know that for a fact, because I tried and I was a total mess. It's one thing for me to be battling depression for so long, but it pains me to see Joey battling it.

In February we learned that my aunty Eileen was dying and so my mom went to Kelowna, B.C. to spend a few days with her and my Uncle Sonny. My mom had flown down to Kelowna and since Cory and Gigi wanted her to spend a few days with them too, they drove to Kelowna to pick her up. That way she could spend a few days with them and fly home from Vancouver. She taught them how to make perogies while she was there and they took her around seeing the sights. Gigi's family made mom feel really welcome and she very much enjoyed her visit with them.

The fundraising social for the foundation was planned for February 13. I wanted to make it a really good social so that people would have a good time and it could possibly have become an annual event. I collected over 100 prizes for the silent auction, the buy an envelope thing, and for door prizes. I hired a live band and an Elvis impersonator. The problem was, I just couldn't sell enough tickets. By the time I paid for the hall rental, the live band, the Elvis impersonator, and all the other incidentals I was more than a thousand dollars in the hole. I had printed 400+ tickets and sold less than a hundred. When it got to be the day of the social there was still a lot of people who had tickets out and I had no idea how many tickets were actually sold, so I just kept hoping. I had also hoped that there would be a whole bunch of people wanting tickets on the night of the event because that often happens, but not in this case.

The people that did come had a really good time and pretty much everybody won something and that was nice. However, it was very hard to hold in my disappointment. I managed to hold it in most of the night and then when it came time to pay for the hall rental, the band, and all that stuff, I couldn't hold back the tears any longer. I had put so much time and effort into that fundraiser and I failed. I don't know what else I could've done to sell more tickets. I thought that I did plenty enough advertising and I had given quite a few people tickets to sell, they just weren't selling. I had left 100 tickets at the high school in Ste. Anne that we give the scholarships to and when I went there to find out how many were sold, I was devastated to learn that not one single ticket was sold. This was something I was doing for the students of Ste. Anne Collegiate, yet they had not sold one single ticket.

I expressed my feelings of disappointment to the school

afterwards and they apologized and said that the school had so many fundraisers and that they had never done fundraising for another organization before. This wasn't really simply for another organization though, because ultimately it was the students at their school that would benefit. I guess that I expected or hoped that they would've wanted to be more involved. Who knows though, it was the first year for the scholarships and awards and maybe not enough people were aware of the fundraiser. I thought that I did plenty enough advertising but maybe not. There was also a school basketball tournament going on that weekend so maybe it was bad timing.

I learned a lesson from going in the hole with that fundraiser and that was to keep the overhead lower in the future. If I would've had just a DJ instead of the live band and Elvis impersonator, I would've at least broken even. So I decided to chalk it up as a learning experience and move on.

Just a couple of days after the social my aunty Eileen died and Bob's sister, June died. We didn't go to my Aunty Eileen's service in B.C. but my mom was glad that she had gone and spent time with Aunty Eileen before she died. Even though Aunty Eileen had been sick for quite some time and her death was expected, I was deeply saddened by her passing. I had grown to love her very much over the years. We went to June's service which was held in Winnipeg at Chapel Lawn Cemetery. June at age 58, was the eldest of Bob's sisters (4th eldest of 13 siblings). Her death was sudden and unexpected. We were never really that close but June was one of those people that were at the hospital right away showing her care and concern when I had my tragic accident. So although we didn't see each other much, she was Bob's sister and we were saddened by her death. I was sad for her husband and children and knew that they'd have a hard time dealing with their loss.

After June's funeral, I was reading the paper and realized that somebody else very dear to us had died. It was Matt Kotowicz's mother, Pearl Kotowicz. She was the dearest, sweetest, lady that I'd ever met. I had really grown to love her and it saddened me that I missed her funeral. I had heard from Matt's son, Lee that she was not doing too well in the hospital and I kept meaning to go there and see her. I wish that I hadn't kept putting it off, for now it was too late. Matt and Elaine were there so much for me, after my accident and I felt really bad because I didn't make it to the funeral. I went over to see them and express my sympathies. I told them that I didn't hear about the funeral in time to go, otherwise I would have.

Cory and I had been communicating back and forth about his upcoming wedding. I wanted to do more but it was their wedding and they wanted to do things their way. I think that the groom's parents are usually less involved than the bride's anyway, but I was excited and I wanted to be more involved with this important day in his life. There's an old saying, "A son is a son until he takes a wife, but a daughter is a daughter for the rest of her life." I started thinking about that saying and realized how true it was. Then I realized how I would never know the joys of planning a wedding with your daughter, and Stacey would never meet, nor marry the man of her dreams.

Cory knew that I was feeling left out and wanted to be more involved so he did allow me to do a couple of things. He let me get some personalized mint cards and scrolls made up to hand out as souvenirs. I had also requested that the guys all wear a daisy boutonniere in memory of, and out of respect for Stacey and he agreed to that. I would have liked to throw a wedding shower for Gigi too, but since they were in Vancouver and I was here, that wouldn't have worked out.

Cory asked Joey to be his best man and of course Joey accepted. Joey had recently got himself a suit because he needed it for presentations at university, which would do fine for the wedding. I bought a silver and burgundy Asian dress. I thought they were so pretty and I had always wanted one; now it seemed the perfect opportunity. My mom found a lovely mauve dress that looked really good on her. Bob is not the type of guy who wears suits, so I got him some grey dress pants and a burgundy shirt.

My nephew Kris had also proposed to his girlfriend, Stacey and she accepted. Their wedding was planned for July 31, 2004. They would be getting married in Winnipeg, and of course we were invited. Kris was doing quite well at his job, working at an insurance company. Through his work he was taking courses which would one day lead to his accreditation as an insurance broker. Stacey was about to graduate from a legal assistant course. They were very much in love, and we were very happy for them.

For my next fundraiser for the foundation I planned to get teddy bears made so that we could sell them. I found the owner of "Kibby Bears" to be quite helpful. She gave me a lot of helpful hints and ideas. Together we came up with a nine inch lavender bear, which we called "Stacey's Hope". The bear had our yellow ribbon of hope with a daisy on its chest and a hang tag attached. I was quite excited about them and couldn't wait to see the finished product.

Since it was going to be six years since the accident in May, MPIC decided that they wanted to know where we were going as far as rehabilitation was concerned with me. Should they continue with the intense therapy that I was receiving, or was I as good as I was going to get? Actually, it was a question that was on the minds of everyone involved with my treatment, myself included. They scheduled me to go for all kinds of testing and would make a decision based upon the outcome.

At that time I was seeing my family doctor on a biweekly basis for treatment and follow-up care of my accident related injuries, which still involved the Fibromyalgia/ Chronic Fatigue Syndrome, the permanent nerve damage and related arm and shoulder deficits, memory and other cognitive difficulties related to the brain injury, poor sleeping related to the depression and guilt over the accident and subsequent death of my daughter, as well as post-traumatic stress disorder. I was also seeing a psychologist and life skills coach on a weekly basis and a psychiatrist on a monthly basis. Due to my decreased ability to function on a physical and cognitive level, I had also been receiving home care assistance which provided some of the necessary help that I required to do household chores.

The testing was intense and very exhausting. The outcome wasn't really surprising to me because I kind of knew what I was and wasn't capable of. They had decided that I had reached a plateau and any further progress would be very minimal. I would never be able to return to nursing and as far as learning new things goes, they said that I'd be capable of learning simple, task oriented things. For example, if I were to become a diabetic and needed to use a glucometer to test my blood sugar, I'd be able to learn that.

Before we knew it Cory's wedding was upon us. Stacey's friend, Amy decided to come to the wedding in Vancouver with us. Neither her nor Bob had ever been on a plane before and they were both pretty excited about it. The flights, hotel, and car rental were all booked using my Airmiles - thank goodness for Airmiles!

The wedding was beautiful; the ceremony was done in both Chinese and English. The pastor that Cory and Gigi had in Winnipeg actually drove all the way to B.C. to perform the ceremony. That was pretty special.

Before the actual wedding ceremony, Cory and Gigi performed some of the traditional Chinese customs, like the tea ceremony. The Chinese Wedding Tea Ceremony is an important ceremony for all Chinese newlyweds. It is usually done without any qualms as it is symbolic of paying respects to your in-laws and elders. Tea is China's national drink and serving it is a sign of respect. Using tea is also practical, because not everyone can drink alcohol.

Lotus seeds and two red dates are used in the tea for two reasons. First, the words "lotus, year, seed, child, date, and early" are homophones, meaning they have the same sound but different meanings in Chinese. Secondly, the ancient Chinese believed that putting these items in the tea would help the newlyweds produce children early in their marriage and for many years thereafter, which would ensure many grandchildren for their parents. Also, the sweetness of the special tea signifies the sweet relationship the bride wishes to have with her new family.

The tea ceremony began at the home of Gigi's parents. This is done out of respect and to thank her parents for raising her. Gigi's elders were then invited to share tea with them, one at a time beginning with the eldest. The general rule is to have the woman on the left side and the man on the right side. The people being served the tea will sit in chairs, while the bride and groom kneel. The bride and groom serve the tea by holding the teacups with both hands and inviting the people to share tea with them, addressing them by title. In return the bride and groom receive lucky red envelopes ("lai see", which means lucky) stuffed with money or jewellery.

Next Cory and Gigi came to our hotel room to perform the tea ceremony with us. It was really quite interesting. They served the tea in order, beginning with Bob and I (the groom's parents) and then proceeded from the oldest family members to the youngest. One thing I found interesting was that the tea could not be served to anyone younger than them and the people younger than them are not allowed to give them a red envelope. Yeah, so Joey and Amy could not be served tea, nor could they give Cory and Gigi a lucky red envelope.

It was truly a wonderful wedding and we were so grateful to be able to share that very special day in their lives with them. The only thing that would've made it better is if Stacey were there. She would've absolutely loved to be there at Cory's wedding! I am glad that Amy came along though because she was a part of Stacey's life too, and it helped to feel closer to Stacey. I think that it'll always be hard to go through these kinds of things without Stacey and there are still times when I put on my "plastic face" and tell people what they want to hear; because it's easier.

The sixth anniversary of Stacey's death was only a week after Cory's wedding. I planned to be spending that milestone a little differently than usual. I had planned to do another fundraiser for the foundation which involved holding a double session bingo, to be held on the sixth anniversary of the accident.

Attendance for the event was lower than we anticipated and we ended up in the red. Not being one to give up easily, and since we still had lots of bingo paper and break-opens left, we decided to try and run a weekly bingo. We were hoping to recoup the money that we had to put out to purchase the bingo paper and break-opens. We thought, or at least hoped, that if we could increase awareness that there was a weekly fundraising bingo in the community more people would start coming.

My sister-in-law Ellen Pchajek, designed some beautiful ceramic Circle of Angels candle holders for us to sell as a fundraiser for the foundation. She did all the work making them out of the goodness of her heart; the only thing that she charged me was what it cost her to make them. The first two that she made we raffled at the bingo; one at each of the two sessions. They were simply breath-taking! She made them lavender with a glistening sandstone finish to co-ordinate with our teddy bear, Stacey's Hope. After that though, we thought that as beautiful as the lavender was, it just might not match the décor in some people's homes. With that in mind, we began offering them for sale in the buyer's choice of colors.

The teddy bears arrived just in time for the double session bingo. I thought that we'd sell more at the bingo than we did, but most of the teddy bear sales have been aside from the bingo. Rolande's Gift Shop in Ste. Anne, Hallmark Card & Gift Shop in Steinbach, and Pumpkin Pastimes Teahouse in Anola, were all kind enough to assist us by selling Stacey's Hope in their place of business.

We also did a "Home & Gift" fundraiser in May and that went pretty well. Some people that I hadn't seen in awhile came or at least called to place an order and that was nice. My girlfriend Carol placed a good sized order and I hadn't seen her in a couple of years. I've known her since we were both twelve years old and so we've been pretty close. Also, her daughter Alia was very good friends with Stacey. Carol had been very supportive to me after the accident but in past couple of years she had some difficulties of her own to deal with. Her friendship means a lot to me and I'm really glad to have her back in my life. We ended up making about three hundred dollars from the "Home & Gift" fundraiser and I was pretty happy with that … it was definitely better than going in the hole!

Another fundraiser that we did in May and June of 2004 was the "Colossal Closet Clear-out". This didn't involve any selling and it benefited our organization, the Canadian Diabetes Association, and needy families. Bins were place at Ste. Anne Elementary School and letters were sent out asking people to clean their closets of clothing that they no longer wanted or needed. Condition of the clothing was not a factor as anything that the Canadian Diabetes couldn't sell in their thrift stores was recycled. Even though we didn't make a lot of money of it, I really liked that fundraiser because so many people benefited.

The first annual Stacey Pchajek Memorial Awards were coming up and it wasn't hard to select a winner because only one person from grade eight and one person from grade twelve were nominated. It was a little disappointing that only one person from each category was nominated but it was only the first year for the awards.

I wanted to be there to present the awards myself at both schools but as it turned out, the grade eight awards night fell on the same night that Sylvia Browne (the psychic) was going to be in Winnipeg. As soon as mom and I heard that she was going to be in Winnipeg we booked our tickets. We decided that wouldn't be a problem because Bob and Amy could present the grade eight award.

Mom and I were really excited to go see Sylvia Browne in person and I was hoping and hoping that I'd get a message from Stacey. The place was packed and she did a really good show, but I did not get a message from Stacey. I was somewhat disappointed but I told myself that it was probably important to everyone who went there and she couldn't possibly give everyone a reading. I could tell that it was very important to those who did get the readings. I had really wanted to be one of those people getting a reading, but I wasn't and that was okay. We were still really glad that we went and enjoyed the show.

Bob and Amy were really nervous presenting the award and forgot to get a picture. We were able to give the grade eight recipient a bouquet of daisies, Stacey's Hope (our teddy bear), a copy of the book that Stacey's "Friendship" poem was published in called "Theatre of the Mind", a graduation pin, a $100.00 gift certificate, and a plaque. The girl who received the award was very deserving, and Bob and Amy said that she was delighted upon presentation.

The First Annual Stacey Pchajek Memorial Award for grade twelve not only went to a very deserving student, but also one of Stacey's very best friends, Vanessa Joe. Vanessa received a bouquet of daisies, a copy of "Theatre of the Mind", a graduation pin, a plaque, and a scholarship for $800.00. Presenting the award to Vanessa was a very emotional moment for both her and me. I didn't quite get the picture that I wanted to publish because we both just sort of stood there crying and hugging each other for a very long time.

Vanessa and Stacey first became friends through figure skating. Stacey was a couple of years older than Vanessa but they soon became inseparable. They shared a very special bond … and they always will.

Our family went to the dinner and dance for the Ste. Anne Collegiate graduation as well. It was an awesome meal and everyone looked so nice. It was really hard to see how all these guys and gals had grown and become mature young adults though; especially since they were all a couple of years younger than Stacey. It was yet another reminder that the world was going on, without our precious Stacey. I still thought of most them the way that I remembered them when Stacey was still alive. I expected them to still look like that, but they didn't.

My nephew T.J. Pchajek (Darlyne & Fred's son) graduated that June as well. Since T.J. was also a couple of years younger than Stacey, I experienced those same feelings and emotions at his ceremony about the world going on without Stacey. I really wanted to be happy for T.J., Vanessa, and the others but at the same time I felt such a deep sadness and hollowness.

Since the accident, for the most part I was apathetic. I didn't really care about much of anything; much less get excited over anything. However, when I heard that psychic John Edward was coming to Canada for two shows I was simply ecstatic! He was going to be doing one show in Saskatoon and one in Toronto. Saskatoon was only a 10-12 hour drive and mom was willing to go with me, so we booked our tickets right away. My Aunty Eleanor's birthday was on the same day as the John Edward seminar (July 9th) and since she lived less than an hour away from Saskatoon we decided to meet there in Saskatoon. Once again my Airmiles came in handy to book our hotel room. Aunty Eleanor was going to meet us there at the hotel, we'd spend the weekend there in Saskatoon, stop at my sister's in Moose Jaw, and then Aunty Eleanor would come home with us. She planned to visit with us for about a month in total and then fly home.

I was absolutely thrilled to be sitting there in the audience of the John Edward seminar, at floor level. Once again though, I had my hopes up for getting a personal reading. I kept thinking, "Please Stacey, please come through". I said those words to myself and aloud many, many times … but she didn't. I was so sad because I wanted to hear from her so bad. Was she out there watching us? Could she see us there? Could she hear me begging her to come through? Didn't she know how much that I desperately needed to hear from her? These questions and so many more kept going through my mind. But, just like when we went to see Sylvia Browne, I realized that not everyone in attendance can get a reading. Maybe next time, I hope!

At the end of July, we went to Kris & Stacey's wedding. It was a real nice wedding and we were glad that we were able to share the day with them. It was easier attending their wedding without Stacey than it was Cory's though. I was missing her there though and requested a special song from the DJ to be played in Stacey's memory. That song was, "All my Life" by KC and JoJo.

When my nephew John heard the song start playing, he knew that I must've requested it and he came and asked me to dance with him.

It's a beautiful song, and if you've never heard it before here are the lyrics:

All My Life
by KC and JoJo*

I will never find another lover sweeter than you, sweeter than you
I will never find another lover more precious than you, more
precious than you
Girl You are Close to me you're like my mother,
Close to me you're like my father,
Close to me you're like my sister,
Close to me you're like my brother
You are the only one my everything and for you this song I sing

All my life I pray for someone like you
I thank God that I, that I finally found you
All my life I pray for someone like you
I hope that you feel the same way too
Yes, I pray that you do, love me too

Said I promised to never fall in love with a stranger,
You're all I'm thinking of I praise the Lord above,
For sending me your love, I cherish every hug,
I REALLY LOVE YOU!!!

All my life, I pray for someone like you,
I thank God that I, that I finally found you
All my life I pray for someone like you
I hope that you feel the same way too
Yes, I pray that you do, love me

You're all that I've ever known, your smile on your face, all I see is
a glow,
You turned my life around, You picked me up when I was down,
You're all that I've ever known, when you smile your face glows,
You picked me up when I was down
You're all that I've ever known, when you smile your face glows,
You picked me up when I was down & I hope that you feel the

same way too,
Yes I pray that you do love me too

All my life, I pray for someone like you,
I thank God that I, that I finally found you
All my life I pray for someone like you
I hope that you feel the same way too
Yes, I pray that you do, love me too
All my life I pray for someone like you

Joey tried returning to university in the fall of 2004 but he wasn't ready. At first it seemed like he was going to be okay but his inability to focus or concentrate soon became more and more of a problem. By October, he was feeling very frustrated and overwhelmed and he had to drop out. I felt so bad for him and at the same time I felt so helpless because I couldn't make things better for him. I could be there to offer support, encouragement and guidance, but it was him that would have to work though it and it wasn't going to be easy.

The weekly bingo that we started as a fundraiser for the foundation was not going so good. We tried increasing our advertising, "Bring a Friend" and membership incentives but despite our best efforts we just kept going further in the hole. In October we met with the Manitoba Gaming Control Commission and they saw no other alternative but for us to stop running the bingo. We gave it our best effort though and that's what counts. We appreciated the fact that Ross Community Club donated the use of the hall, and we appreciated the regulars who came out every week to show their support.

The next fundraiser that I planned was a "Bud Spud'N Steak" at Tijuana Yacht Club in Winnipeg. It was held in October of 2004 and it was thrilling to finally have a successful fundraising event!

We made over a thousand dollars that night and it was a lot of fun too. Stacey's friend Alia Furtado, sang a very special song in Stacey's memory.

The song was called "One Sweet Day" and here are the lyrics:

One Sweet Day
Mariah Carey feat. Boyz II Men*

Sorry I never told you
All I wanted to say
And now it's too late to hold you
'Cause you've flown away
So far away

Never had I imagined
Living without your smile
Feeling and knowing you hear me
It keeps me alive
Alive

And I know you're shining down on me from heaven
Like so many friends we've lost along the way
And I know eventually we'll be together
Together
One sweet day
Eventually I'll see you in heaven

Darling, I never showed you
Assumed you'd always be there
I took your presence for granted
But I always cared
And I miss the love we shared

And I know you're shining down on me from heaven
Like so many friends we've lost along the way
And I know eventually we'll be together
One sweet day
Eventually I'll see you in heaven
Although the sun will never shine the same
I'll always look to a brighter day
Lord I know when I lay me down to sleep

You will always listen as I pray

And I know you're shining down on me from heaven
Like so many friends we've lost along the way
And I know eventually we'll be together
One sweet day

Those beautiful lyrics, together with Alia's beautiful voice had many of us in tears. Her song added such a special touch to the evening, and I just know that Stacey was shining down on us all that night.

Other fundraisers that we did in 2004 included selling mom's home-made pies and perogies, and Christmas dainties. We also did a couple of raffles which turned out okay. The foundation has become very important to me and I'd eventually like to get enough funds to start an endowment fund so that we wouldn't have to fundraise so heavily each year. It would also be nice if I could get enough funds to give scholarships at more schools in our area. Eventually, I'd like to open it up to all of the schools in Manitoba. That would be nice.

All lyrics are property and copyright of their owners. All lyrics provided for educational purposes only.

Cory and Gigi's Wedding

In this picture, Gigi is wearing the red Chinese dress that she wore for the Chinese Tea Ceremony. Left to Right: Gigi, Cory, Joey, Doreen, Bob, & Grandma (my mom)

Joey at Cory's wedding

Stacey's Hope

Circle of Angels

Vanessa Joe going to receive award.

Vanessa receiving the first annual Stacey Pchajek Memorial Fund
award was very emotional for both of us.

CHAPTER TWENTY

HERE AND NOW

In January I contacted my cousin, Etta in England for the very first time. It's been really good finding out more about my dad's family and where my dad came from. I think that going through the loss of a child strongly influences and reinforces the value of family in a very powerful way. When I hear people complain about their troublesome teenage son or daughter, I just want to tell them that those problems are nothing compared to what they'd be going through without that child in their lives. Embrace every moment and realize that some things are just not that important.

Another thing that I noticed is that I have a strong need to complete things. It's kind of like the old adage, "Don't put off til tomorrow what you can do today". I guess it's because you are well aware that you or one of your loved ones may not be here tomorrow. You become intensely aware of the possibility of your own mortality or of losing another loved one. To a greater degree than ever before, you find yourself stopping and thinking, "What if these were the last words that I shared with this person?"

On February 13 I started writing this book. I had always enjoyed writing before and my kids thought that I was good at it. They (especially Stacey) were always telling me that I should write a book. In the back of my mind I always thought that one day I would. Finally, I decided that it might be a good idea to share with people what it's like to experience the "Ultimate Tragedy".

I've come a long way since that fateful day; but I still have a long way to go. The road is rocky, and there are many pot holes. There are still times that I'd love to go back to being that person that I was, with the life that I had; but instead the only thing I can do is move forward. That's all that any of us can do. Well that's not entirely true I guess; because there are people who simply become stagnant, forever mourning and grieving their loss. As much as I rejected and fought off the change though, I knew that if I were to remain stagnant I would be doing a great injustice to my surviving loved ones. At times, it seems as though I'm not making any progress but if I look back at how I was a year ago, I can see that I've made progress. The changes are small and gradual so you cannot look back over a week, or even a month to see the difference. But if you look back to a year prior, you'll realize that you have made some progress.

Cory continues his battle with Attention Deficit Disorder (ADD) and I really feel for him because it's got to be so frustrating for him. Getting married and starting off in a married life are very stressful events and as I mentioned earlier, stress impacts both his Gilberts Syndrome and the ADD in a very negative way. Can you imagine what it would be like to have the channels in your mind constantly changing? It gets so bad that you are unable to concentrate or focus on anything. It must be so frustrating for Gigi too.

To a person who doesn't know or understand about ADD, it might appear as though Cory is being lazy because he's not able to attend to simple daily tasks when the ADD is out of control. Although Gigi is trying to be patient and understanding, I know how frustrating it can be. It's hard enough for a young couple starting out their life together and the ADD makes it that much harder. Their love is strong though so I'm confident that their marriage will survive. He's been trying new medications but so far none of them have had much effect. Right now though, he is able to function in day to day activities as well as at his job so he's happy about that. However, he wants to be the best husband that he can be for Gigi so he is still seeking a treatment that will help to keep his condition more stable and I'm glad for that.

On a very positive note, Cory's Crohn's Disease seems to be much better since he's been eating mostly Asian food. I don't know if eating mostly Asian food would help everyone with Crohn's Disease but it sure agrees with Cory. Asians eat a lot of fish and a lot of greens and not really anything fried or fatty so I can see how it would be healthier. Asians are also not very big on desserts, something that most of us North Americans tend to overindulge on. Come to think of it, our family does eat a lot of desserts ...I wonder if that impacted negatively on Cory's Crohn's Disease? That could very well be, because now that Cory is married to Gigi he doesn't eat much desserts and his Crohn's is better. I haven't really done much research to see how much of a role diet plays with Crohn's Disease but with Cory, at least for now, it seems to have played a major role.

Stacey's friend Whitney is attending the University of Lethbridge on a hockey scholarship this year and in February she came to Winnipeg to play against the University of Manitoba. A bunch of us got together to go watch her play and then we all went to Boston Pizza after the game. It was really nice to see Whitney and everyone again but at the same time it hurt and I got this hollow feeling; because Stacey should've been there. I love all of these girls dearly and I hope that they'll always want to have a relationship with me and my family; but at the same time it's hard to watch them all growing up and realizing their hopes and dreams while Stacey cannot. As hard as it is though, it would be much harder if I didn't have them in my life. I love it that they include me and share their joys as well as their disappointments with me.

One of Stacey's very good friends was very close with me in the beginning and then sometime in 2002 she just stopped calling and coming around. I tried on a number of occasions to contact her but she never returned my calls. I don't understand what happened because I loved her dearly and thought of her as a daughter. I was sure that she cared a lot about me and my family and I just don't know what could've caused her to break off communications. I have heard from other people that she is doing well, so that's good but I'll always wonder about her and her family. I cared a lot about her whole family and when I just stopped hearing from them I wondered what I could've done. Did I smother her, trying to get her to take Stacey's place without realizing I was doing it? Was I too depressing to be around? I only wish that I knew. Losing the friendship of this dear sweet girl, her siblings, and her mother has been very hard and I miss not having them in my life. Her mother was very special to me too and I truly valued her friendship. If they are reading this, they'll know who they are and I'd like them to know that I'm so grateful to have known them and they will be forever in my thoughts and in my heart.

Even though Joey had dropped out of school in October of

2004, he didn't stop learning. He started self-teaching himself many valuable computer skills. By learning these things through reading and tutorials at home, he could work at his own pace and without pressure. We were glad that he was at least doing something valuable with his time but he was not getting out in the world and socializing. We felt that he was spending too much time at home on the computer, which isn't really that healthy. There was also the fact that he tended to stay up all night on the computer and sleep all day.

In February Joey applied for a term position with Canada Revenue Agency. After submitting his application he received a call to go in and write a test, which would assist them in the selection process. It took close to six weeks to receive the test results but he ended up doing quite well. He was glad and we were all very happy for him. Of course, not as happy as we all were when he got the job! He not only needed the money but he needed to get back into a routine and out into the world again. He has only been on the job for a week so far but it has made such a wonderful difference in him already. For the first time in a while he seems happy and hopeful again. Getting this job at this point in time is the best thing that could've happened to him and we are all so thrilled for him. He is saying that he hopes to do really well at the job and get his term extended. It is totally awesome to see him being confident and thinking positive again!

One of the things that Joey was teaching himself in the past couple of months was "HTML" meaning Hyper Text Markup Language. A "HTML" file is a text file containing small markup tags which tell the web browser how to display a page. It is an important thing to learn for making websites. When Joey made the first website for the foundation he used a program called "Microsoft Publisher". It's a good program if you don't know a lot about building a website and it does a nice job. The problem was that a lot of it (like the pictures) could only be viewed by people using "Internet Explorer" as their browser. It also seemed to use a lot of space making your website larger than necessary and slower at loading. So anyway, just before starting his job at taxation he redid the website using html.

It was also about the same time that we decided to do a fundraiser with "Charmingly Yours" selling their Italian style charms and bracelets so he uploaded all of their charms and bracelets to the website under "fundraisers". We also wanted to get a custom charm with our logo on but neither Joey nor I was entirely happy with the logo; the daisy just didn't look enough like a daisy. So Joey refined the logo again and we are quite happy with it now. The website looks absolutely gorgeous now; he did a superb job! It's still not quite finished because there are still more things he wants to do to it; but that's the way websites are, you are constantly updating them.

Mom has been keeping her high blood pressure pretty well under control with the aid of diet and medications. Her osteoarthritis gives her mild to moderate discomfort which has been somewhat more bothersome since going off the Vioxx (which was the cox 2 inhibitor, anti-inflammatory drug that was banned here in Canada). Ironically enough, shortly after going off the Vioxx, mom started having problems with plantar fasciitis and heel spurs. I think that it's either ironic or coincidental because Vioxx was one of the main drugs prescribed for plantar fasciitis and heel spurs. Although mom was taking the Vioxx for her osteoarthritis maybe they never realized that she had the plantar faciitis and heel spurs before because the Vioox was masking the symptoms. That makes perfect sense to me.

"Plantar" refers to the bottom of your foot; "fascia" is a connective tissue that holds the muscle in place; "itis" simply means inflammation; so plantar fasciitis means that the bottom of your foot is inflamed. Heel spurs are deposits of calcium that occur when there is tension and inflammation in the plantar fascia attachment to the heel. The plantar fascia, which is the connective tissue that holds the muscles in the sole of your foot in place, supports the arch of the foot and connects the ball of the foot to the heel.

When walking and at the moment the heel of the trailing leg begins to lift off the ground, the plantar fascia endures tension that is approximately two times body weight. This moment of maximum tension is increased if there is any lack of flexibility in the calf muscles and/or if the person is overweight; the more overweight a person is, the more the tension is increased. Usually the pain is felt in the front and bottom of the heel, but it can be anywhere on the bottom of your foot. The intensity of pain can be anywhere from mild to severe; often becoming debilitating. It is usually intermittent, meaning that it comes and goes in varying degrees of severity every few months or years for the rest of a person's life. The exacerbations can last anywhere from a week to several wceks. I have already mentioned that lack of flexibility in the calf muscles and being overweight can cause this condition; other causes are: increased activities such as being on the feet too long, having improper arch support, or wearing shoes that don't bend easily under the ball of the foot and/or have little cushion on hard surfaces. Due to the repetitive nature of walking, plantar fasciitis may be a repetitive stress disorder similar to tennis elbow. Both conditions benefit greatly from rest, ice, and stretching. Surgery is usually a last resort because it can often do more harm than good in up to fifty percent of the patients.

Mom just got over one very debilitating episode of plantar fasciitis which lasted for a good ten days. She couldn't stand or walk for those ten days; all she could do was rest and take ibuprofen. Her doctor now wants her to go and see about getting an orthotic made for her sure to see if that will help.

I still depend on my mom for a lot of support and I think I'd be lost without her. She is my best friend and a constant source of motivation. I am so grateful to have such a wonderful and loving mother who is so caring and understanding. Besides providing me with emotional support and encouragement, she helps me with the foundation, my housework, and so much more!

Bob continues to keep busy, both at work and at home. He always seems to have some kind of project going on. His most recent project involved fixing up an old snowmobile that he found at the dump. The thing really looked like a piece of junk when he brought it home, but by the time he finished with it you wouldn't have known that it was the same machine. He not only gave it a shiny yellow paint job but he painted orangey-red flames on the front and both sides of it. He is very talented but I think that he even surprised himself with how good he was able to make that snowmobile look.

He also has a couple of older Ford Broncos that he plans to fix up mechanically and paint. He is planning on painting flames on the broncos as well and since he had never done it before he thought that the snowmobile would be a good thing to practice on to see what kind of a job he could do. Since the snowmobile turned out good, he feels more confident about painting the flames on the broncos now. On the next page you will see before and after pictures of his snowmobile.

Before

After

He is definitely a man of many talents! Basically he can do anything that he sets his mind to do, and quite well I might add. He loves to do anything mechanical, including rebuilding engines. He can also do plumbing, electrical, drywall, carpentry, you name it!

One thing that I'd really like is to get our renovations done. We started renovating a few months before the accident and after Stacey's death things just kind of came to a standstill for awhile due to lack of motivation. It's almost seven years now, and although we have gotten some of the renovations completed there is still a fair amount to be completed. For the most part now though it's due to a lack of funds as opposed to lack of motivation. I am so tired of not having a kitchen. I mean it's great that we have mom's kitchen to use, but I want my own kitchen to use. It's mainly just the kitchen and dining room that need to be done but the kitchen is very costly, especially since at present we have no cupboards. Ours were really old and wrecked so we ripped them out when we started the renovations. In the beginning I had hoped to get some cupboards that would be both nice looking and efficient, but now I just want cupboards and a completed kitchen.

I suppose it's good that I am actually hoping for and wanting something now though, because for the longest time I didn't hope for or want anything other than to have Stacey back in our lives. For a long time Cory said that he hoped that one day my thinking would be less jaded again; I never really knew what he meant by that but I guess that the way I chose to see everything in a negative manner with no hope for the future was part of it.

One thing that hasn't improved is my memory and concentration. It is so totally frustrating! It involves both short, and long term memory. Also, if I'm working on something for the foundation then everything else gets left behind because I can only seem to focus in on one thing at a time. The same goes for when I was writing this book, which was all I could concentrate on so everything else got left behind. Everything else includes many things like housework, laundry, paying bills, and going to appointments. Sometimes I get months behind in the bills and don't realize it until I start getting delinquent and disconnection notices. I feel really bad about it and when you get that far behind it's so hard to catch up, so every time I say that I won't let it happen again but it does. All of these things that I was used to taking care of before with no problem have now become very frustrating for me.

I'm sure that you are all waiting to hear if things have improved in the bedroom yet for Bob and I. Well, the sad truth is not yet. I have been thinking about it more and at times I've actually desired it, but then I get afraid. I think that I'm getting less afraid of moving on without Stacey, and more okay with me experiencing pleasure again though.

Now, I think I'm worried more about how much it'll hurt, and if I initiate something will I be able to follow through? Those are positive changes that lead me to have hope. There was a time when I didn't see any possible way that we could ever be sexually intimate again, but now that possibility exists. It's taken me almost seven years to get to this stage and Bob has stuck by me every step of the way. I love him deeply and there is no doubt in my mind that he feels the same about me.

CHAPTER TWENTY-ONE

FOR THE BEREAVED PARENT

The death of a child is the ultimate tragedy that any parent will ever face in their lifetime. It defies that natural order of things; everyone knows that children are not "supposed" to die before their parents. Parents are also "supposed" to protect their children from all harm. This sense of responsibility leads to a devastating sense of guilt when the death of a child occurs. Even if everything that could've been done for the child was done you still feel as though you failed as a parent. Even if there was nothing that you could've done to prevent the child's death, or it was purely accidental, the self-blame and guilt persist in an agonizing way.

While it is normal to experience these feelings, you need to be careful to not be so consumed with guilt that it becomes anger turned inward. That happens when you unconsciously become so angry at the situation that you internalize all your feelings of anger and guilt. That can lead to severe depression and is also physically unhealthy. I know about this from firsthand experience, as I myself internalized my feelings of guilt and anger.

They say it helps to talk about it and realize that if others can hear and accept what you have or have not done; you will be more able to accept the fact that you did the best you could at that particular time, which is all anyone can do. However, I also know from experience that forgiving oneself is far more difficult than forgiving someone else. We are harder on ourselves than we are on others, that's for sure. My suggestion is that if you are experiencing overwhelming or prolonged feelings of guilt; seek help through support groups, therapists, and/or psychologists. Please do not let it consume you, because it will literally eat away at you.

Although bereaved parents share many of the same thoughts and feelings, the experience is different for everyone. There is no "right way" to grieve and there are no time limits. Only you will know what helps and what doesn't help. You will no doubtlessly encounter people who will tell you how you "should" grieve; don't listen to them. It was your child that died and it's your grief, not theirs. Sure, it's important to move forward but I think that you shouldn't take on more than you think you can handle; grieve and move forward at your own pace.

In the first year following the death of your child you will experience many new and strange feelings. You may experience intense pain, feelings of unreality, isolation, exhaustion, fear, panic, sleeplessness, loss of appetite or overeating, headaches, stomach upsets, depression or overwhelming feelings of sadness and hopelessness, loneliness, emptiness, guilt, anger, decreased concentration, sexual difficulties, and a general feeling of losing control. Hallucinations as in seeing the dead child are not uncommon either.

As you can see, many reactions can occur. Sometimes people might even feel as though they are losing their mind but these are all common reactions to grief after the death of a child. Again though, I caution that if your feelings start becoming too overwhelming or intense seek help through support groups, therapists, psychologists or even a minister or priest at a church can be helpful.

As alone as you might feel in your grief, you need to keep in mind that you are not the only one grieving. Other family members and friends have been affected by the child's death too. Each family member's perception of the death may be different and there may be feelings of ambivalence, anger, love, resentment, and more. Try and be understanding of each other's feelings.

Children's reactions will vary according to their age. Until the age of two they have no concept of death; from age two to four death is regarded as a temporary situation; at ages four to six death is sometimes viewed as a punishment for wrong-doings; from age six and on they are developing an adult concept of death as being that of permanence. Children in the family need to know that you love them and it can be helpful to share thoughts and tears with them. They need to know that it is okay to feel sad and angry. Young children may also think it was their fault that their sibling died because they had "wished" them dead sometime shortly before the death. They may have said something like "I wish you were dead" to them out of anger, and then truly believe that it was them that caused the death. Another thing to be careful of with children is not to say things like "he or she is gone to sleep, or has gone to heaven to be with God" because the child might then be fearful of going to sleep and or fearful of God taking them away from their parents.

Husbands and wives usually grieve quite differently from each other too and this can lead to problems. While one spouse might find it easier to keep busy and not talk much, the other might find they need to talk and cry lots. Normally, when a husband and wife are faced with difficulties they face them together, but with the loss of a child it's different. Each partner is struggling so hard with their own grief that they just don't seem to have anything left for anyone else. Society still expects men to be the strong one too and that can further complicate the grieving process for many men.

Learn to accept and respect each other's methods of grieving even if you don't understand it. Give each other the necessary time and space to heal. If your spouse is having a bad day, say you are sorry and that you understand but don't try to get him or her out of their mood; allow them to feel. This doesn't mean stop communicating; you still need to do that. Although you each need to grieve in your own way, you still need each other very much.

It is also a difficult time for grandparents, other family members, and friends as well. They are unsure of how to act around you and they worry that they might say the wrong thing. Actually, there are people that do say the wrong things but try to take what they say with a grain of salt. Most people mean well and are not out to hurt you, they just sometimes say something without thinking or realizing that it could be taken in a hurtful way.

One that really bothered me was when someone would say, "Well, it was her time dear." I wanted to scream at them, "What the heck do you mean it was her time? She was thirteen years old for crying out loud!" You'll hear all kinds though: "God never gives us more than he thinks you can handle", "Well at least you have other children", "I know just how you feel, I lost my 90 year old grandma last year". Usually family and friends want to help but don't know how. If there is some specific way that you could use their help, come right out and ask them. Don't be afraid to be direct and specific.

Grief places a tremendous amount of stress on the body and consumes all of your energy. All of this stress also weakens your immune system, making you more susceptible to a host of illnesses. Although you may not feel much like eating and sleep may be difficult, both are vital to your physical and emotional well-being. Taking care of yourself will not likely be one of your priorities but it's important.

Remember that if your grief is so profound that you are finding it difficult to function, see your doctor. If a depression develops secondary to the grief, it may need to be treated in order for you to deal with the grief. Another important piece of advice is not to try and lessen the pain with alcohol or non-prescription drugs. Learn to work through your hurt, rather than mask it.   .

CHAPTER TWENTY-TWO

HOW TO HELP A GRIEVING PARENT

Grief is a natural and normal response to a loss. It is painful, confusing, isolating, and lasts much longer than society recognizes. Professionals have tried to place timetables on grief based on their studies. Many of them quote "two years" as the normal grieving period; but those of us that have been down that road will tell you that it takes much longer. There is no real timetable on grief; it's different for everyone.

Grief is a process, or a moving through. You may have heard that there are stages in the grieving process: denial, anger, bargaining, depression, and acceptance. The thing is, we don't go through the stages in an orderly fashion. It's not like you can say, "She's in stage three now, so just two more stages to go." That would be too simple. Instead, we move all over through the stages. Sometimes we move forward, sometimes we go backward, and sometimes we get stuck for awhile.

Grieving parents are facing the ultimate tragedy, which is the worst tragedy that they will ever face in their lifetime and they need all the support that they can get. Many people say that they don't know what to say to a parent who has just lost their child. The fact is, there are no magic words that one can say to ease the pain. "I am so sorry" is really all that anyone can say.

What you don't want to say are things like: "I know just how you are feeling", because you don't; and please don't say, "It was his/her time" … we are talking about children who had their whole lives ahead of them.

If you find yourself at a loss for words, you really don't need to say anything. A simple hug and just being there to listen can do wonders. The grieving parent needs to talk about their loss and you can help by allowing them to express their thoughts and feelings in a non-judgemental manner. Allow them to cry, be angry, and express their feelings of guilt or shock and disbelief.

Another way that you can help is by preparing a meal for them. The last thing they feel like doing is cooking and in their grief they may forget to eat. Grieving takes a lot of energy and food provides energy. Other things that I found very helpful were when someone came over and tidied up, did some laundry, or ran some errands. Helping out with the other children is another way that you can help.

Remember the child's birthday or anniversary of their death with a card, phone call or visit. Also remember that the parent will be experiencing many firsts without their child. It helps to know that others are thinking of them and their child during these difficult times. This can include: Back to School, Halloween, Thanksgiving, Christmas, and Easter.

Another thing that I found helpful was communicating with close friends and family through email. Most people, including myself, find it easier to express their thoughts and feelings in writing as opposed to in person.

Remember that the surviving siblings are grieving too, and their feelings need to be recognized as well. Some people brought my kids cards, stuffed toys, books and angels. Age appropriate books to help them understand their grief are another good idea.

CHAPTER TWENTY-THREE

SECOND EDITION UPDATE

It's now 2015, ten years since I wrote the first edition of Ultimate Tragedy. A lot has happened since then and I felt that an update would be appropriate. I'm sure that you are all wondering about many things.

The first question that I usually get asked is, "Did you ever get your kitchen?" Well the answer to that is a very emphatic "Yes!" In 2008 I won the bonanza jackpot at Giroux Bingo for $12,548. I only needed two numbers after the pre-call and I had never been that close before. I just had the feeling that they were going to be the first two numbers out and they were! After being without a kitchen for ten years I knew exactly where my share of the winnings was going. My mom and I always shared our winnings at bingo but six grand was still pretty awesome. The ironic part was that Bob and I had just made an appointment at the bank to borrow money to get the kitchen done. We were worried if we'd get approved for the loan but now that we had the six thousand dollars things were looking much more positive. As it turned out we got the loan and I now have a beautiful kitchen and a dining room.

My mom is turning eighty-eight this year and she continues to be a very important part of our lives. She is such a remarkable woman and I'm so grateful to have her here in our lives. We have cut back on making and selling the pies, perogies, etc. for fundraising. As you can imagine it was a lot of work for both of us and with mom getting up there in age I thought that we needed to do some other fundraising that wasn't so much work. Our main fundraiser now is a weekly bingo in Richer, Manitoba. It is going very well with a good attendance. Mom runs the canteen there and she does a fantastic job.

Everyone is always anxious to see what homemade goodies she has each week. They especially love her homemade cinnamon buns and pies.

We have a great group of volunteers at the bingo and I appreciate all the help of each and every one of them. This year we will be giving out our very first Volunteer Scholarship to Caitlin Leclerc. She has been volunteering with us for the past three years, since grade ten. I asked her if she will stop volunteering after she graduates this year and her reply was, "Oh no way, I love it here!"

Over the past ten years the Stacey Pchajek Memorial Foundation has given twenty-two grade twelve scholarships and ten grade eight awards. I think that is pretty fantastic and Stacey would be so very proud. I'm still working on getting enough money to start an endowment fund but we are getting much closer to achieving that goal. The problem that I have is that there are so many deserving nominations and they are all so good that it's hard to narrow it down to just one or two. In the beginning it was much easier as there were less nominations but each year there are more and more nominations and the students are so totally amazing. I am finding that there are not only more students graduating compared to ten years ago but the students are doing so much more. They are more involved with their community and are very innovative. They are constantly pursuing ways to help others and be the best person they can be.

SPMF (Stacey Pchajek Memorial Foundation) also does what we can to help other organizations. We are a big supporter of local Christmas hampers because we believe that no one should go without at Christmas. We also donate to the Cancer Society, Siloam Mission and other local organizations.

Cory and Gigi have been living in Hong Kong for the past ten years. He comes home to visit but we have never been there. He still struggles with his ADD (Attention Deficit Disorder) and I feel bad for him as I know that he is having a hard time. As a mother I wish I could make everything better but all I can do is offer my love and support. It's hard to do that though when he is living so far away. They have not had any children yet; which is probably a good thing since I would rarely get to see them. Okay, maybe that is being a bit selfish but if and when I have grandchildren I would really like to be a big part of their lives.

I am very proud to say that Joey graduated from the University of Manitoba with a Computer Science degree in 2011. Since then he has been working for the IT department of Canada Revenue Agency. He and Bob are very close and they like to go hunting and fishing together. They also both have handguns and like going to the gun range. I'm very thankful that they have such a close relationship and so many similar interests. I used to hope that he would meet that special girl and fall in love but now I just want him to be happy. He definitely seems to be happy now and he looks forward to doing things that he enjoys so that is good.

Stacey's friends and cousins are all getting married, having careers and having kids. That is nice, but it's also hard for me to see them fulfilling their hopes and dreams knowing that Stacey can never do that. I feel so guilty like it's all my fault that Stacey can't be here to fulfill her hopes and dreams. I wonder if she would have become a teacher like she wanted. I wonder if she would have travelled like some of her friends. I wonder if she would have fallen in love and got married. I wonder if she would have had kids by now. Don't get me wrong; I'm happy for all her cousins and friends. I'm just sad that Stacey couldn't do all the things that they are doing.

In 2006 Bob had a small stroke which he fully recovered from. He is still taking the Plavix and low dose aspirin but only as a precaution. We were all very glad that he didn't have any permanent deficits or problems. It was scary when it happened, but thankfully he made a very speedy recovery. It could have been a lot worse but I think that maybe Stacey was looking out for us. She knew how much we all need and love him and I have to believe that she is there watching over us.

Now the part that you've all been wondering. In 2008 Bob and I finally started having sex again! I'm telling you it was like being a virgin all over again, if you know what I mean. It was Dr. Dyck that really got everything started. I was at one of my complete physicals when he could tell that we still weren't having sex. He asked me if I talked to Bob about my feelings in regards to being afraid to have sex. I told him "No, but he knows why." He said, "Don't assume, you need to talk to him about it." So I got up the courage to talk to Bob and he knew that pain was a big part of my reason but he didn't really understand everything until I talked to him about it. I'm so grateful for his patience but I now understand that Dr. Dyck was right, "Don't assume". When we did start having sex again I first had to overcome the fear but Bob took it slow and waited for me to be ready. Then it became wonderful and it was like two teenagers who couldn't get enough of each other. We became so much closer than ever before.

In 2009 I did something that I never thought I would accomplish; I quit smoking! I did it with the help of Champix and Bob was so happy and proud of me. One of the first things you notice after quitting is the smell or rather the stink. I used to smoke in my house all the time and I was a two pack a day smoker but I never realized how bad it made the house smell until after I quit. In fact, it was probably about a year after I quit that I was in the home of two people that were heavy smokers and that's when it hit me. I thought wow that must've been what my house smelled like. I did put on some weight when I quit and I didn't really like that. People said that it was good to see me put some weight on but when I went from being ninety-five pounds to one hundred and fifteen I was like whoa, that's enough. I did try going to Curves for awhile but it was just too difficult with my fibromyalgia. Lately my weight fluctuates between one hundred and five to one hundred and ten so that's not too bad.

In June of 2010 we went on our first ever Alaskan Cruise. It was our first vacation since 1996 when we took the kids to BC. My mom had always wanted to go on an Alaskan cruise and we were so delighted to be able to take her. It was only for a week but we had such a great time. It was so relaxing and the scenery was amazing. Bob and Joey did some really neat excursions like going in a helicopter and landing on a glacier. Mom and I chose to do something else while they were doing that but we also did excursions that all four of us could do. The food and entertainment on the ship was fabulous and I think that we really needed that vacation. I did have my periods when I felt so bad that Stacey wasn't there but I think in spirit she was.

In the fall of 2010 I had to have bladder surgery due to stress and urge incontinence. What they did was insert a mid-urethral sling. During the procedure they nicked my bladder so I had to go home with a catheter. That was only for about a week though. The surgeon said that would fix part of my problem but I would still have to take the Vesicare for the other part of the problem. After a couple of weeks we tried to have sex again and the pain was excruciating. It felt like I was being ripped apart and we had to stop. Every time we tried after that it was the same thing. There was no possible way that we could do it even if I tried to put the pain aside. It was just too excruciating and it did not matter how much lubricant we used either. I went to Dr. Dyck about it and he sent me back to the urologist. The urologist checked the sling and said that it was in place like it should be so the problem must be gynecological. Dr. Dyck sent me for an ultrasound after that and did a pelvic exam. He thought that I might have pelvic congestion syndrome and gave me things to try. Nothing worked and to this day we have been unable to have sex again. I still think that the sling is to blame and if I had to do it over again I would never have had that surgery. I have heard that other people have had problems like this after having a sling put in and there are lawsuits pending right now for a lot of people.

The meds that I'm on for my depression are keeping it under control for the most part. However, I find myself wanting to be alone a lot lately and I have a tendency to be more apathetic. I'm also tired most of the time but that is probably a combination of the depression, my meds and the fibromyalgia. I also have had enough of winter; maybe I need another vacation.

ABOUT THE AUTHOR

Doreen Pchajek is a former nurse from Ste. Anne, Manitoba. She is the founder/chairperson of Stacey Pchajek Memorial Foundation Inc, which is a nonprofit, charitable organization that provides scholarships, bursaries, and prizes to students graduating grades 8 and 12 in southeast Manitoba.

In 1998 Doreen was faced with the Ultimate Tragedy, which is the greatest tragedy that any parent can ever face; the death of her only daughter. This experience has changed her life forevermore. She decided to write about her life altering experience in the hopes that it could help others who are faced with a similar tragedy and give others a better understanding of what the bereaved parent goes through.

Made in the USA
Charleston, SC
27 March 2015